edexcel

ging lives

Edexcel GCSE
Business Studies
Introduction to Small Business

Teacher Guide

Alain Anderton • Ian Gunn

Andrew Ashwin consultant editor

A PEARSON COMPANY

Acknowledgements

Published by Pearson Education Limited, a company incorporated in England and Wales, having its registered office at Edinburgh Gate, Harlow, Essex, CM20 2JE. Registered company number: 872828

Edexcel is a registered trade mark of Edexcel Limited

Text © Alain Anderton, Andrew Ashwin, Ian Gunn 2009

First published 2009

12 11 10 09

10 9 8 7 6 5 4 3 2 1

British Library Cataloguing in Publication Data

A catalogue record for this book is available from the British Library

ISBN 978 1 846906 053

Edited by Dave Gray

Proof reading by Sue Oliver, Mike Kidson

Artwork by Matthew and Caroline Waring-Collins

Designed by Steve Moulds

Printed by Ashford Colour Press Ltd., Gosport

Cover image by © Getty Images/Martin Mistretta

Every effort has been made to contact copyright holders of material reproduced in this book. Any omissions will be rectified in subsequent printings if notice is given to the publishers.

Websites

The websites used in this book were correct and up to date at the time of publication. It is essential for tutors to preview each website before using it in class so as to ensure that the URL is still accurate, relevant and appropriate. We suggest that tutors bookmark useful websites and consider enabling students to access them through the school/college intranet.

Disclaimer

This material has been published on behalf of Edexcel and offers high-quality support for the delivery of Edexcel qualifications.

This does not mean that the material is essential to achieve any Edexcel qualification, nor does it mean that it is the only suitable material available to support any Edexcel qualification. Edexcel material will not be used verbatim in setting any Edexcel examination or assessment. Any resource lists produced by Edexcel shall include this and other appropriate resources.

Copies of official specifications for all Edexcel qualifications may be found on the Edexcel website: www.edexcel.com

Welcome to the Teacher Guide

Topics and Chapters

Scheme of work

Welcome to the
Edexcel GCSE Business Studies Teacher Guide
Introduction to Small Business

Covering the EDEXCEL specification

This Teacher Guide and CD-ROM have been written to fully support the:

- GCSE Business Studies;
- GCSE Business Communications;
- GCSE Business Studies and Economics;
- GCSE Short Course in Business Studies;
- specifications from September 2009.

GCSE in Business (all pathways)

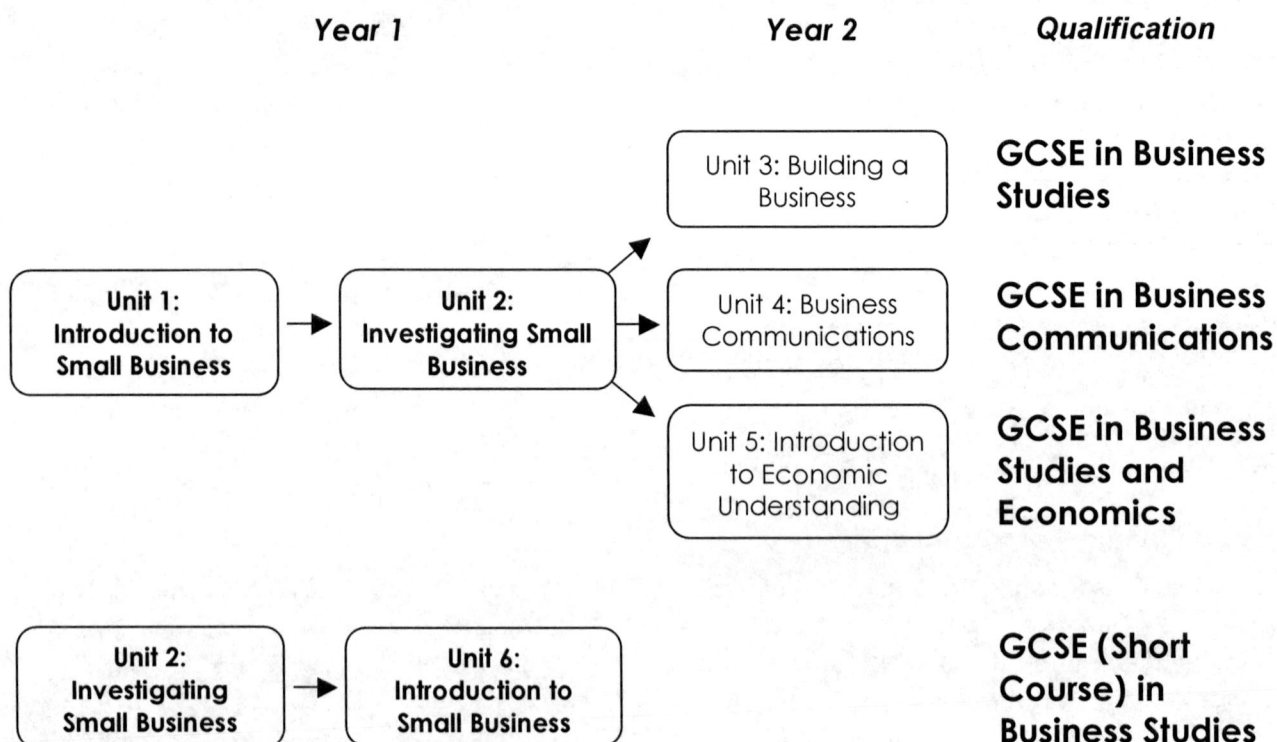

	Year 1	Year 2	Qualification
		Unit 3: Building a Business	**GCSE in Business Studies**
	Unit 1: Introduction to Small Business → Unit 2: Investigating Small Business	Unit 4: Business Communications	**GCSE in Business Communications**
		Unit 5: Introduction to Economic Understanding	**GCSE in Business Studies and Economics**
	Unit 2: Investigating Small Business → Unit 6: Introduction to Small Business		**GCSE (Short Course) in Business Studies**

Delivering the EDEXCEL specification

GCSE qualifications in business subjects encourage students to be challenged and follow a broad course of study. By using the materials in the student book '**Introduction to Small Business**' and this **Teacher Guide** you will be equipped to help your students to achieve the best they can. Through completing the Topics set out in these books your students should be well on their way to achieving GCSE or be completing their short course.

This Teacher's Guide includes materials for the following Units from the specification:

Unit 1 concentrates on the key issues and skills involved in enterprise. It provides a framework to consider the marketing, financial, human and operational issues involved in starting and running a small business.

Unit 2 encourages students to research, analyse and evaluate a selected task on enterprise issues.

Unit 6 is an introduction to small business and forms part of the compulsory material to achieve the GCSE (Short Course) in Business Studies.

Inside the Teacher Guide

Inside this Teacher Guide is support for you to teach the Units in the Edexcel GCSE Business: Introduction to Small Business student book by Alain Anderton and Ian Gunn. It includes:

- a complete **Scheme of work** that follows the structure of the book for you to organise your course.

- **suggested answers and mark schemes** that provide comprehensive support for you and your students on the assessment included in the student book.

Scheme of work

The scheme of work provides a guide to teaching the course over 28 weeks. It gives suggested activities for each part of the course. These are linked to the resources available in the chapters of the student book and the resources in the ActiveTeach. Other resources that are available and might be used are also suggested. The scheme of work gives the option of following the plan set out, or using it to come up with new ideas to deliver the specification.

Suggested answers and mark schemes

Suggested answers are provided for all questions in the student book.

Topic overview: A case study sets the scene for each topic, accompanied by a series of questions. They might be used as a starter activity to find out what students already know about the subject. Suggested answers or discussion points are given for each of the questions that are asked.

Test yourself: The answers are provided for the objective test questions in each chapter. The reasons why the answers are correct and why others are incorrect are explained, helping students understand why they are getting answers right or wrong

Over to you: The answers and mark schemes for the examination-type Over to you questions are provided. They reflect the marks allocated to questions in the exam and the mark schemes that are used, helping to understand how examiners mark answers. Showing students how marks are given will help to improve answers and grades.

Exam zone – Practice exam questions: These give the student the opportunity to take a 'mini exam' at the end of a topic. The questions, answers and mark schemes reflect those that appear in exams. Getting to know how marks are given will help students to improve answers and grades.

Review questions: There are 10 short answer questions for each chapter and 10 suggested answers. They could be used at the end of lessons or for homework to find out if students have understood that area of the course or as revision before an exam.

The Teacher Guide CD-ROM

Material on the Teacher Guide CD-ROM is fully customisable giving you complete flexibility with the questions, answers, mark schemes and scheme of work. It also means you have the ability to make the materials available to your students to use an ICT suite, or at home.

Navigating the CD-ROM

Once you have run the CD-ROM or installed it, you will then have the option of viewing and using all the resources in the printed Teacher Guide.

To navigate the CD-ROM, simply click through the folder links until you reach the resource you are looking for. Actual resources are indicated by a specific icon.

The resources are arranged according to the topics and chapters of the student book.

On the first page you will find a link to the scheme of work, along with links to each topic.

Within each topic folder you will find links through to the individual chapters and the following resources:
- Topic overview
- Practice exam question

Within each chapter folder you will find the following resources:
- Test yourself
- Over to you
- Review questions

Opening resources

To open any of the resources simply click on the link and, if you have the minimum required software, the material will open in an external programme.

Breadcrumb trail

Backward navigation of the CD-ROM is achieved by means of a 'breadcrumb trail', found at the base of each menu screen. As you navigate through the levels of options within the resource browser, a trail develops at the bottom of the screen. You can retrace your steps by clicking on the various elements of the breadcrumb trail to return to a specific screen. Pressing the 'Menu' link at the start of the breadcrumb trail will take you back to the main menu screen.

Further Information

At the bottom of the resource browser window you will find links that open information on troubleshooting and on the licence.

Running/installing the CD-ROM

You have four options to run this software, accessed when you put the CD in the CD drive and it autoruns.

- **Run.** This happens automatically when the CD is put into the drive. It allows users to access the software direct from the CD.
  With this option you will always need the CD in your computer.

The following three options require the user to select the 'install' button at the bottom of the screen when it autoruns.

- Install it to a **single PC**/laptop – local install.
  All files are installed onto the PC and the software runs without the CD in the drive.

- Install it to a **network**. The software is organised for network distribution. Subsequently the software then runs without needing the CD in the CD drive.

- Install it to a **VLE**.

Note: If the CD fails to autorun, open the CD folder, click RB.exe and proceed as above as desired.

Case study

Kristen Lockey had worked for her father's building company for ten years. Now, she wanted to go it alone and start her own business. She didn't want to compete directly with her father's company. So she looked around for a different line of business. After much research, she came up with the idea of setting up a business specialising in building conservatories, verandas and decking.

Her father's company had already done a few jobs installing conservatories. Kristen knew that there was a good market out there. However, she didn't want to compete directly with the big companies in the market. They advertised heavily and had large numbers of people in sales, promoting their products. Kristen saw, though, there was a gap in the market for one-off, specially designed conservatories and decking. These would be made with the best materials. So Kristen would be able to charge her customers a high price for a product which had a lot of value added. High quality both of the product and of service would be the unique selling points for the business.

In her research, Kristen looked at whether there were any franchising opportunities available in the manufacture of conservatories. Taking on a franchise could help her establish her own business. However, she couldn't find anything that looked suitable. So she decided that she would have to set up in business on her own.

Suggested discussion points/answers

1. Why are the needs of customers important for the success of Kristen Lockey's new business?

Possible needs could include:

- has gone for a specific gap – customers who want high quality
- their needs and her USP match up
- market oriented product
- custom-built/made to measure
- unique designs

2. Explain why Kristen Lockey decided to make 'one-off, specially designed' conservatories.

Possible reasons could include:

- gap in the market
- has done some research to find this out
- no franchises suitable
- no competition
- did not want to compete with father
- bigger companies did not meet customer needs

3. Why might an entrepreneur looking to set up a new business consider a franchise?

Possible reasons could include:

- Known brand
- Tried and tested
- Training
- Adverts
- Equipment
- On-going products
- On-going support
- Advice
- Exclusive area
- May have better market knowledge

Chapter 1: Businesses

1.   What is the purpose of a business?

Select **one** answer.

A   To give everyone a job

B   To make big profits for its owners

C   To produce goods and services

D   To pay taxes to the government

Answer C

Comments
A Incorrect – job creation is a by-product of business.
B Incorrect – this is an objective.
C Correct – it is the primary purpose of business.
D Incorrect – businesses do not want to pay taxes.

2.   A small business makes cakes for parties and weddings. Which **two** of the following are most likely to be resources it uses directly in production?

Select **two** of the following.

A   Labour

B   Taxes

C   Television adverts

D   Flour

E   Airfreight

Answer A and D

Comments
A Incorrect – labour is needed to operate machinery. It is one of the resources used in the production of cakes.
B Incorrect – taxes represent a flow of money out from the business not a resource used in production.
C Incorrect – adverts do not make anything.
D Correct – it is a raw material – an ingredient used in cake manufacture.
E Incorrect – it is a possible cost.

3. Justin Terrett is a professional DJ who travels to engagements in his van with all his kit. Which **two** of the following are most likely to be suppliers to his business?
    Select **two** of the following.

    A   A club renting his services

    B   A television company running an article about his business

    C   A local petrol garage

    D   The individuals who attend the gigs he does

    E   Record stores

Answer C and E

Comments
A Incorrect – they are hiring his services and therefore represent a demand for his product.
B Incorrect – the television company is advertising his product through the programme and not supplying him with anything.
C Correct – he needs petrol to get to engagements. The garage is supplying him with a product to enable him to carry out his business.
D Incorrect – he supplies them not the other way round – they pay for the service he provides.
E Correct – the records are part of the resources for his business.

Chapter 1: Businesses

The Jayne Varndall Motorcycle School prepares motorcyclists for their riding tests. To ride a motorcycle, you need to have a specialist driving licence which is different to one for driving a car or a lorry. Jayne Varndall, the owner, employs four people: a secretary and administrator and three instructors. She has an office and a large car park that she uses to instruct motorcyclists at the start of their training. Her business has operated for the past ten years.

Jayne's customers pay for a basic instruction course in riding a bike. Then they are charged by the hour for on-road practice before taking their test at a local government centre. For their training, they can either hire a motorbike from him or bring their own bike. The market for motorcycle instruction is competitive. There are three other businesses in the area that offer similar services. There used to be four, but one business closed down because it couldn't get enough customers.

1. 'Jayne Varndall provides a service to her customers.' What is meant by 'a service' and 'customers' for Jayne Varndall's business? (4)

Indicative content
Service

- Non-physical product
- Something the customer cannot provide
- Usually requires special skills

Customer

- Someone who buys the product offered
- Someone wanting to learn to ride a bike

Mark scheme
A definition is given for 'service' and for 'customers' (1 mark for each). An example of each is given for Jayne Varndall's business (1 mark for each).
For example, 'Customers are people or organisations that buy or are supplied with products by businesses. Customers of Jayne Varndall's business are people who pay for the product she provides – basic instruction in riding a bike'.

2. Identify and explain how **two** resources are used by Jayne Varndall to produce the service she provides. (8)

Indicative content

- Labour
- Equipment
- Materials

Mark scheme
1 mark for each appropriate resource given, up to a maximum of 2 marks. There are 3 marks available for each explanation of how the resource is used by the business. For example, 'Jayne Varndall's business uses labour (1 mark). Labour is the workers in a business. There are five people who work in the business. (1 mark) Jayne, the owner, will control the business, but she employees three other workers. One of these acts as a secretary, handling administration, such as paying bills. There other workers are instructors, providing lessons. (1 mark)

3.   'One business closed down because it could not get enough customers'. Giving reasons for your answer, analyse **two** possible reasons why Jayne Varndall's business has managed to survive against the competition for six years. (6)

Indicative content

- Experienced
- Other business have closed down
- Good facilities
- Good pass rate
- Reputation
- Location
- Good prices
- Understands customer needs
- Knows its market well

Mark scheme

Level	Mark	Descriptor
	No mark	Non-rewardable material
Level 1	1–2	Simple statement with no/limited supporting explanation. For example, 'The business has survived because of the skills of the instructors in the business.'
Level 2	3–6	Reasons are given and explained. For example, 'The business has survived for six years as a result of its reputation. It may have developed a good reputation as a result of the skills of its instructors. They could be experienced and get good pass rates for customers. Customers could then recommend the business to others. Local media may also report on its success. These factors will attract further customers, making the business profitable.' This would be worth 6 marks.

Chapter 1: **Businesses**

1   What is meant by the term 'market'? Give an example of a market.

2   What is meant by the term 'supplier'?

3   State four examples of types of goods that might be supplied to a supermarket.

4   State four examples of raw materials.

5   What is the difference between a customer and a consumer?

6   Give an example of where a customer and a consumer are the same and an example of where they are different.

7   What is meant by a 'business opportunity'?

8   State two threats to any new business.

9   'Selling the service was the easy part. It was all the legal bits that caused me problems.' State three examples of the 'legal bits' that businesses have to take into account.

10 What is meant by the term 'production'?

Suggested answers

1   A market is where buyers and sellers meet to agree a price. An estate agent sells houses and flats to people who want to buy houses and flats (the housing market). Steel producers sell steel to construction companies and manufacturing companies who want to buy steel to use in their businesses (the market for steel). A clothing shop sells clothes to customers (the retail clothing market).

2   A supplier is a business that sells or supplies products to other businesses.

3   Examples of types of goods are fruit (oranges, apples, bananas etc.), meat (chicken, steak, port etc.), drinks (Coca-Cola, orange, wine, water etc.) and breakfast cereal (Corn Flakes, Weetabix, Cheerios etc.)

    Examples of services are dry cleaning, banking, paper delivery and bus transport.

4   Examples of raw materials are wheat, oil, coal and fruit, although there are many others.

5   A customer is the person or organisation buying a product. A consumer is the person who ultimately uses the product.

6   Same – someone who buys and eats a pizza for lunch.

    Different – someone who pays for the contract on a mobile phone which is then used by someone else.

7   A business opportunity is a chance to take advantage of a gap in the market where demand is not being met at present. This could be happen, for example, if there is a change in fashions, if an existing business ceases operation or if a new product is wanted and is not currently provided.

8   Examples of threats could be competition, a lack of demand, a lack of cash and legal issues.

9   Examples include following Health and Safety guidelines to make sure the workplace is safe for staff and customers, paying the correct taxes on time, such as National Insurance, and VAT, and ensuring all paperwork is correctly maintained so that appropriate government departments can check records when needed, e.g. employment records.

10 This is where resources such as raw materials, labour and equipment are bought and used to make products. The resources used will vary from business to business and from product to product.

Chapter 2: **Understanding customer needs**

1. Chris wants to set up a business fitting kitchens and looks in *Yellow Pages* (a commercial telephone directory) to see what others businesses offer similar services in his area. This is an example of what type of research?

   Select **one** answer.

   A   Qualitative

   B   Primary

   C   Secondary

   D   Observation

   Answer C

Comments
A Incorrect – this refers to the type of data collected not the type of research.
B Incorrect – the information was collected and processed by someone else.
C Correct – the information was collected and processed by someone else (the people who compile *Yellow Pages*).
D Incorrect – observation is a method of market research.

2. Which **one** of the following is a type of primary research?

   A   Conducting a survey

   B   Analysing past sales figures of other businesses

   C   Reading market reports

   D   Consulting local newspapers

   Answer A

Comments
A Correct – it is collecting data first hand with a focus in mind.
B Incorrect – the information already exists so it is secondary.
C incorrect – the data has already been processed by somebody else so it is secondary.
D Incorrect – the newspaper is a collection of articles complied by someone else and can be looked at historically so is secondary research.

3. Which two of the following are most likely to give a researcher qualitative data?

Select **two** answers.

A   The meeting of a focus group

B   Researching names of businesses in an area from a telephone directory

C   Researching the products made by competitors by looking at internet sites

D   Conducting interviews with shoppers in a supermarket

E   Analysing government statistics

Answer A and D

Comments
A Correct – the purpose of a focus group is to gather opinions.
B Incorrect – these are facts not data to be processed.
C Incorrect – these are facts which do not tell the researcher anything about why people buy.
D Correct – it tells the researcher about consumers' opinions.
E Incorrect – these data are quantitative.

Chapter 2: **Understanding customer needs**

Grace and Peter Fletcher had always made fabulous cakes. Their friends knew this and often, when picking up children from school, they would be asked to make a cake for a child's birthday party. As their children got older, they began to think that they could turn their cake making skills into a proper business.

Grace and Peter took their time to research the market. They had kept records and photographs of all the cakes made for other people. They analysed these to see what sort of cakes were popular and how much they had charged. Going to their local supermarket, they saw what special cakes were available on the shelves. For several Saturdays in a row, they spent an hour in the cake aisle noting down who bought these special cakes. They used the local telephone directory, *Yellow Pages* and *Thomson Local Directory* to see who offered cake making services in the local area. They rang all the local suppliers to get a quote on a cake, so that they could see what prices the potential competition charged. They also looked in their local newspaper to see if cake makers paid for advertisements and what sort of adverts they placed.

During this period of research, when they made a cake for someone else, they would make a second small cake exactly the same. They would invite their friends round for a cup of coffee and a piece of the second cake. This was so they could listen to their opinions about cakes.

1. Explain what is meant by 'primary research'. In your answer, give **two** examples of primary research used by Grace and Peter Fletcher? (6)

Indicative content

- Collected by the business needing it, for a specific purpose
- Original data, not collected before for any other reason
- First hand
- Observation
- Survey of competitors
- Surveys of consumers
- Focus group

Mark scheme

An appropriate definition is given (up to 2 marks). Two appropriate qualities are identified and explained (maximum 2 marks for each). For example, Primary research is the gathering of new information, called primary data, for a specific purpose. (1 mark) This is original data that has not been collected before, for any other reason. (1 mark) One example of primary research used by Grace and Peter is observation. (1 mark) They waited for an hour in the cake aisle of a supermarket to see how customers behaved. (1 mark) Another example is a focus group. (1 mark) They made copies of cakes they had produced and asked friends around to give their opinions. (1 mark)

2. Explain what is meant by 'secondary research'. In your answer, give two examples of secondary research used by Grace and Peter Fletcher. (6)

Indicative content

- Information already in existence
- Data processed by others into information
- May have been someone else's primary data
- *Yellow pages*
- Local newspapers

Mark scheme

An appropriate definition is given (up to 2 marks). Two appropriate examples are identified and explained (maximum 2 marks for each). For example, Secondary research is the gathering of information, called secondary data that is already in existence. (1 mark) This data has already been gathered for some other purpose. (1 mark) One example of secondary research used by Peter and Grace is the use of local directories such as *Thomson* and *Yellow Pages*. (1 mark) They provided lists of cake making businesses in the area. (1 mark) Another example is the use of local newspapers. (1 mark) They provided examples of advertisements by competitors. (1 mark)

3. Do you think that Grace and Peter Fletcher have a good understanding of their customers' needs? Justify your answer.   (6)

Indicative content

Yes

*   Repeat customers

*   Suitable research – primary and secondary

No

*   Not a large sample

*   Original target market has grown older, so may disappear

*   No evidence demand still exists, might have been just friends' market

*   Not tested outside circle of known people (friends)

Mark scheme

Level	Mark	Descriptor
	No mark	Non-rewardable material
Level 1	1–2	Simple statement with no/limited supporting explanation. For example, 'The business has survived because of the skills of the instructors in the business.'
Level 2	3–6	Reasons are given and explained. For example, 'The business has survived for six years as a result of its reputation. It may have developed a good reputation as a result of the skills of its instructors. They could be experienced and get good pass rates for customers. Customers could then recommend the business to others. Local media may also report on its success. These factors will attract further customers, making the business profitable.' This would be worth 6 marks.

Chapter 2: Understanding customer needs

1   What is meant by the term 'market research'?

2   What is meant by the term 'qualitative data'?

3   What is meant by the term 'quantitative data'?

4   State two examples of qualitative data and two examples of quantitative data.

5   What is the function of a questionnaire in market research?

6   Explain why using company reports is an example of secondary research.

7   Explain why observing shoppers in a supermarket on a particular day is an example of primary research.

8   What is a focus group? How might a focus group help a researcher?

9   Explain one advantage to a business of using primary research over secondary research.

10 Explain why someone starting up a business could have a problem if they did not carry out market research.

Suggested answers

1 Market research is the process of gathering data about customers, competitors and market trends using primary and secondary research.

2 Qualitative data are data which are based on opinions, judgements and attitudes.

3 Quantitative data are data which can be expressed as numbers and statistically analysed.

4 Two examples of qualitative data are the opinion that a shop is located in the wrong place and the judgement that a new toy is very safe for young children.

   Two examples of quantitative data are that 80 per cent of people wanted another taxi service in the area and that a car cleaning service cleaned 10 cars in a day.

5 Questionnaires are often used when surveys are carried out. They include a list of questions, which are designed to find out data about respondents' tastes.

6 Secondary research involves compiling information that has already been gathered and already exists. Information in company reports already exists. It may have been gathered by the company to show its profits or sales last year, for example.

7 Primary research is the gathering of new information which has not been collected before. Observing people in a supermarket to find out their shopping habits on a particular day will find out new information about shoppers that could not have been collected before.

8 A focus group is a small group of people that are invited by a researcher to talk about a product so that the researcher can hear their reactions and opinions. Hearing their opinions might help a researcher to decide if a new product is likely to be successful or not.

9 An advantage of primary research over secondary research is that researchers can set their own questions to get the answers they want. Secondary research would involve using data that already exist for some other purpose, which may not be suitable.

10 If someone starting up a new business did not carry out any research they would have no real idea if there was demand for the product, how to price it, who to aim at or where to set up. Research is a way of finding out if the idea will sell. Market research is a way of minimising the risks in setting up and may show that it is not worth setting up at all.

Chapter 3: Market mapping

1. A part of a market that contains a group of buyers with similar characteristics is called a market

    A   map

    B   segment

    C   gap

    D   resource

    Select **one** answer.

    Answer B

Comments
A Incorrect – a map only shows a position relative to other businesses.
B Correct – they form a part of the market which the business targets.
C Incorrect – if there is a gap then there are no buyers yet.
D Incorrect – a resource goes into making the product.

2. A toy manufacturer sells toys which are linked to a popular television programme aimed at 1–4 year olds. It also sells toys aimed at 5–9 year olds. The two age ranges for the toy manufacturer are examples of market

    A   resources

    B   maps

    C   gaps

    D   segments

    Select **one** answer.

    Answer D

Comments
A Incorrect – resources are used to make the product which market segments buy.
B Incorrect – maps are used to identify the business' position in a market.
C Incorrect – gaps show chances but there may be no buyers at present because the needs are not being met.
D Correct – they have clear and defined needs typical of their age.

3. Gracja Boniek is investigating setting up as an independent newsagent. She has drawn up several market maps to help her in her market research. A market map is a visual means of showing

    A   where the business is located

    B   the conclusion of a market survey

    C   where a product is positioned in the market

    D   market segments

    Select **one** answer.

Answer C

Comments
A Incorrect – a market map is not a geographical map.
B Incorrect – these are facts which help her decide what to sell.
C Correct – it tells Gracja how her business compares with other similar businesses.
D Incorrect – Gracja already knows these or will identify them from her research.

Chapter 3: **Market mapping**

Kendrick King trained as a hair stylist. He became the manager of a hair salon at the age of 23 and then decided that he wanted to set up his own salon. He knew there was a gap in the market in his local area because there were no hairdressers for Afro-Caribbeans. There was a significant population of Afro-Caribbeans where he lived, but the nearest Afro-Caribbean salon was several miles away. Kendrick researched the market carefully visiting a number of Afro-Caribbean salons in other areas to find out what services they offered and what prices they charged. Another part of his market research was to ask all his friends about what they would like to see in a salon.

1. 'There is a gap in the market in his local area.' Explain what is meant by a gap in the market, using Kendrick's new salon as an example. (3)

Indicative content

- Lack of provision of a product (good or service)
- Could be product per se or in geographical area
- Opportunity for an entrepreneur
- No hairdressers for Afro-Caribbean locally
- Demand existed in the area

Mark scheme

An appropriate definition is given (1 mark) using examples from Kendrick's new salon (2 marks). For example, 'A gap in the market is a situation where no business is serving the needs of customers for a particular product. (1 mark) There is demand in the local area for an Afro-Caribbean hair stylist, because of the local population in the area. (1 mark) But currently there are no salons that provide this service and cater for their needs so there is a gap in this market'. (1 mark)

2. What features of the market could Kendrick have put on a market map to help him position his product? Explain your answer carefully, drawing a market map to help you. (6)

Indicative content

Two of the following could have been placed on a market map.

- Price
- In-salon services
- Quality of his product
- Experience
- Location
- Size of competitors outlets
- Franchises or independents
- Purely Afro-Caribbean or general
- Image

Mark scheme

Up to 2 marks for identifying features and up to 2 marks for explanation. Up to 2 further marks for drawing the map. For example 'Two features that might have been placed on the market map are location and target market. (2 marks) The target market would vary from targeting Afro-Caribbean customers to general customers. (1 mark) The location would be close to where Kendrick is setting up his salon or elsewhere in the area where this market exists (1 mark). The map below shows the market map and the position of Kendrick's salon, which is close to the Afro-Caribbean market/local area axes'.

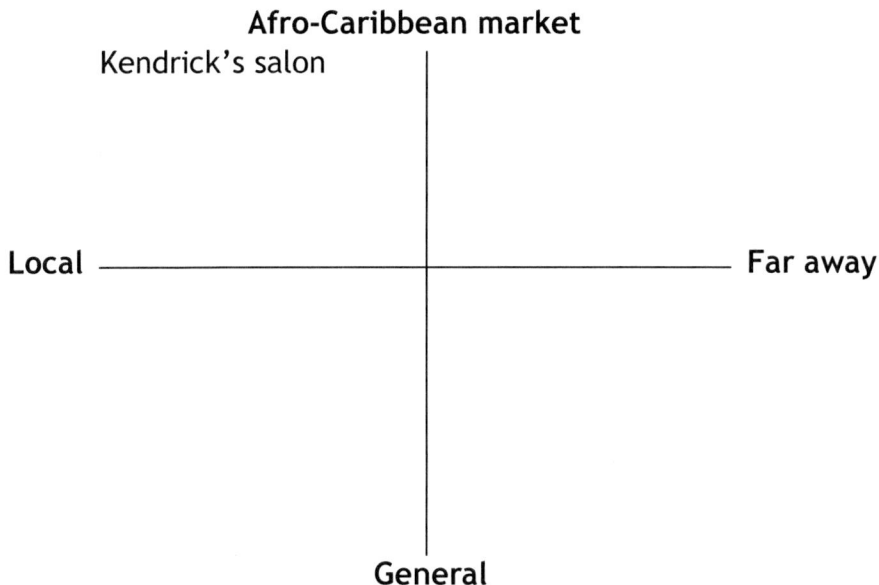

Afro-Caribbean market

Kendrick's salon

Local ———————————————————————— Far away

General

(2 marks)

3. Will spotting a gap in the market guarantee that Kendrick's new business will be successful? Justify your answer. (6)

Indicative content

Yes

- Little competition
- Chances of surviving in early stages
- Chance of building a loyal market if competition does set up
- May take all market – so restrict ability of competition to enter the market.

No

- Never a guarantee of success
- Customer loyalty – may not get effective demand
- No primary research
- Are friends right target market?
- Experience, is his appropriate?
- Quality tested?

Mark scheme

Level	Mark	Descriptor
	No mark	Non-rewardable material
Level 1	1–2	A choice will be made with poorly developed justification and supported by limited examples. For example, 'No, because there is never a guarantee of success in business.'
Level 2	3–4	A choice will be made with some developed justification and supported by some good examples. For example, 'No. There is never a guarantee of success in business. Kendrick's research may not have been accurate. Using family and friends is too limited a sample. When he set the market that he thought might buy his services may not actually use them.'
Level 3	5–6	A choice will be made with a clearly developed justification and supported by excellent examples. For example, 'Spotting a gap in the market may help Kendrick's business to be successful. It may be catering for customer needs that no other business is currently doing. This may help the business to become established and attract loyal customers. However, there is never any guarantee of success. Kendrick may not have researched the market accurately. He may have a good service and loyal customers, but there my not be enough to make the business as profitable as he hoped.'

Chapter 3: Market mapping

1   What is meant by the term 'market segment'?

2   What is a meant by the term 'buying habit'?

3   State four pieces of information that a new car wash might want to find out about its customers.

4   State four ways in which a cinema could split up or segment its market.

5   How does the National Statistics Socio-economic Classification split up the market?

6   Why do businesses want repeat customers?

7   Identify two features that might be put on the axes of a market map of cafes.

8   'A window cleaner has spotted a gap in the market for a house sitting service while people are on holiday.' Explain what this means.

9   Explain two ways in which a new taxi service could find out what its potential customers might want.

10 A market map of clothing shops in a town shows the different types of clothes they sell and the prices they charge. Explain how this market map might help a new clothing shop.

Suggested answers

1 A market segment is a part of the market that contains a group of buyers with similar buying habits.

2 A buying habit is the usual pattern of behaviour that people have when they buy goods or services.

3 Pieces of information might include who its customers might be, what services they might want, what price they would pay, how often they would visit, when they would visit, how far they would be prepared to travel.

4 Methods include by age, gender, income, area they live, ethnicity, families and couples or singles.

5 The National Statistic Socio-economic Classification classifies people according to their type of occupation.

6 Repeat customers are people who come back again and again to buy the products of a business. They spend regularly and provide income for the business. Businesses can rely on them to earn revenue.

7 Features might include price, type of food, location and type of customer.

8 A gap in the market exists where no current business is currently serving the needs of customers. There is a chance that a business can take advantage of this and become profitable, by setting up to provide the goods and services that customers need. In this case no business is currently providing a house sitting service, where a trusted person will guard the house while people are away.

9 One method could be to carry out a survey. This involves asking customers questions about the type of service that they want. Their answers will provide ideas about how the needs of customers can be met by the new taxi service.

A second method could be to observe customers of other taxi businesses. Looking at how they operate and how people use the service could give the business ideas. It might find ways of improving on the service provided by other taxi firms.

10 The market map shows the position of clothing shops compared to each other in terms of the clothes they sell and the prices they charge. By placing itself on the map the business can see how it compares to other shops. Will it have higher or lower prices? Will it sell clothes for younger or older people? The business may be able to identify a gap in the market, for instance if no other shop is selling at a low price to older people.

Chapter 4: Competition

Read the passage below carefully and then answer questions 1 and 2 that relate to the passage.

Tyler's is a small independent shoe store. It is located in a small local high street. A new hypermarket that sells shoes as part of its product offering has just been built at the bottom of the high street. Tyler's has seen its sales fall in recent months and the owner is looking at ways he can compete more effectively.

1. Which **two** of the following methods are most likely to help reduce Tyler's costs in an effort to compete more effectively?

   Select **two** answers.

   A   Increase its advertising in the local newspaper

   B   Provide better service by taking on more staff

   C   Increasing the range of its shoes

   D   Ordering cheaper shoes from its suppliers

   E   Making one member of staff redundant in order to be able to offer lower prices

   Answer D and E

Comments
A Incorrect – this will increase his costs.
B Incorrect – this will increase his costs.
C Incorrect – it might increase the costs but will not reduce them.
D Correct – his cost per item (pair of shoes) goes down.
E Correct – he is paying less on wages.

2. Which **two** of the following reasons are the most likely explanation for why Tyler's has lost half its sales since the new hypermarket has been built?

   Select **two** answers.

   A   The hypermarket is a more convenient place for shoppers to buy shoes

   B   The level of customer service has got worse at Tyler's

   C   The average price of shoes at Tyler's has increased

   D   Tyler's has cut its costs by making one of its four staff redundant

   E   The hypermarket offers for sale many of the same styles of shoes as Tyler's

   Answer A and E

Comments
A Correct – customers have the convenience of one-stop shopping and save on transport costs.
B Incorrect – there is no evidence of this.
C Incorrect – there is no evidence of price either way.
D Incorrect – it is not relevant.
E Correct – it is all under one roof so it is easy and convenient.

3. A business makes bottled and canned soft drinks. Which of the following in itself is most likely to make it more competitive against its rivals?

   Select **one** answer.

   A   The employment of two extra workers

   B   An increase in profit compared to last year

   C   The launch of a new range of drinks

   D   A rise in the price of its drinks range

   Answer C

Comments
A Incorrect – it says nothing about how good the workers are.
B Incorrect – it is not relevant.
C Correct – customers will want to try these so the business gets an advantage.
D Incorrect – this will make it less competitive especially if its rivals keep their prices constant.

Chapter 4: **Competition**

Ellie Morgan is currently the manager of a gym in London. The gym is part of a national chain but things are not going well. The number of clients taking out annual subscriptions has fallen. There are also too few clients coming in and paying a one-off entrance fee for a single session. The equipment and the décor are looking tired and rather shabby. Overall, her branch is losing money. Ellie thinks the gym is likely to be closed within the next 12 months by its owners. This is an opportunity for Ellie to take a different path by opening her own business.

She has a good understanding of the local competition. The market is very crowded. There are national chains of gyms like Esporta that offer good facilities and have a good brand image. They can be a little expensive for customers. However, they seem to have a steady flow of customers.

Then there are the small gyms that are owned by a single person. These are often cheaper for customers although their facilities are usually not as good as the national chains.

Finally, there are gyms that are part of a larger business. There are a couple of hotels in her local area that have a gym for their guests. Local people, though, can also use the gym if they pay. There is also a health spa that offers gym facilities. With both the hotels and the health spa, the gym area is fairly small. However, the equipment is well maintained and some customers like the more intimate atmosphere of the facilities.

With such strong competition, Ellie is not sure she would be able to set up a successful gym on her own. It would need far too much money to set it up. Reading around, though, she found a small business in the Midlands that had had special gym equipment manufactured for primary school children. The machines are much smaller than those for adults. The equipment, together with a trainer, is then hired by primary schools or community centres. Ellie could see a gap in the market in London for this service.

1. Identify **four** different way in which gyms compete with each other for customers. (4)

Indicative content

- Facilities – gym
- Facilities – e.g. café on site, salons
- Price
- Brand image
- Convenience
- Atmosphere – gym per se or extended social gathering/decor

Mark scheme
1 mark for each way gyms compete up to a maximum of 4 marks.

2. Analyse why it might be a problem for Ellie to set up a successful gym aimed at adults. (6)

Indicative content

- Start up costs are high – equipment
- Must match facilities offered by competitors
- May have to take out a loan which adds to costs
- May have to promote to match the brand image of competitors
- May have to offer unique features to attract customers away from existing competition
- May have to pay staff high wages to attract them from other businesses

Over to you answers
Topic 1.1: Spotting a business opportunity
BUSINESS

Mark scheme

Level	Mark	Descriptor
	No mark	Non-rewardable material
Level 1	1–2	Simple statement with no/limited supporting explanation. For example, 'It might be difficult because the costs of setting up a new gym for adults are expensive. This is because the equipment is not cheap.'
Level 2	3–4	A statement is given supported by good examples. For example 'The costs of setting up a new gym for adults will be very high. This makes it difficult to set up and compete. The initial set-up costs of a gym, including equipment are high. If this business wants to attract customers from competitors it will also have to spend money to provide similar equipment.
Level 3	5–6	It will be difficult because the competition is often national chains that are already established. To compete Ellie would have to advertise widely to compete with existing brands. This could be very expensive and not possible for a small business like Ellie. She might also have to pay higher wages to attract skilled staff from rivals. This would add to her running costs. Customers will expect the same quality of service as they currently receive, if not better.

3. Do you think that Ellie could make a success of a gym for children? Justify your answer.   (6)

Indicative content

No

- Cannot test the market as equipment not available in her area
- No research done to support the idea
- Could still be expensive to buy
- Would have to consider lots of health and safety issues and licences which could be expensive and time consuming.

Yes

- No competition
- Target market exists
- Has the expertise/experience
- No overheads as she can be the trainer
- Invite several schools in an area to one demonstration, which would cut costs and promote her business.

Mark scheme

Level	Mark	Descriptor
	No mark	Non-rewardable material
Level 1	1–2	A choice will be made with poorly developed justification and supported by limited examples. For example, 'Yes. There is very little competition for a new business.'
Level 2	3–4	A choice will be made with some developed justification and supported by some good examples. For example, 'Yes. There is a gap in the market. There are many other gyms aimed at adults, but few, if any, aimed at children. The market is potentially quite large as there are many children in schools.'
Level 3	5–6	A choice will be made with a clearly developed justification and supported by excellent examples. It is likely that at this level there will be more balance to the answer. It is likely that at this level there will be more balance to the answer. For example, 'There may be problems setting up this business. The costs of specialist equipment could be high and it could be difficult to research the market with few businesses operating. However, there could be a gap in the market that Ellie could fill. There is little competition and Ellie has the skills required. This could give her a real chance of success.'

Chapter 4: **Competition**

1   What is meant by the term 'brand image'?

2   What brand image might businesses want for the following products?
    (a) Helmets for building sites, (b) a club in town centre, (c) a local taxi service.

3   What is meant by the term 'after-sales service'?

4   State two types of after-sales service that could be given by a garage.

5   Explain why a business might want to develop a brand.

6   Using an example, explain the term 'product range' of a business.

7   List two benefits to customers from competition.

8   State three strengths and three weaknesses to a business of opening a small
    independent sports shop.

9   Explain why someone with experience of the coffee trade might set up a
    specialist store.

10 State two reasons why a business might choose to set up a shop near to a rival.

Suggested answers

1   A brand image is the mental picture, idea or impression that consumers have of a product.

2   (a) Safe and reliable products that will protect wearers. (b) A 'cool', exclusive or exciting place for people to spend an evening. (c) A reliable, quick and relatively cheap service compared to that of local rivals.

3   After sales service is the back-up offered by a business to customers after the purchase to ensure they are happy with what they have got, that it is suitable for purpose so that they will buy from them again.

4   Examples include a check that repairs are satisfactory after a few months and a free test.

5   A brand is a way of creating an identity or association between a product or service and customers. A business might want a brand because people often see brands as being different from other products. They can identify them from other products and will often have brand loyalty, buying the same brand many times.

6   A product range is where a business has a group of similar products with many variations (a mix). For example, a manufacturer of electrical equipment such as Panasonic or JVC will have many different variations of televisions in its product range, including plasma and LCD televisions in a variety of screen sizes.

7   Benefits could be more choice, better prices, better service and more offers.

8   Strengths could be locating near to a target market, stocking a specific range of products to suit local needs, having a small range of stock which reduces costs and that the staff may know the target market personally through sports clubs.

   Weaknesses could be that it may find it hard to compete on price with bigger shops, that it may face retaliation, that it may not be able to stock complete product ranges due to space and that it may find advertising is too expensive.

9   Someone with experience of the coffee trade might set up a specialist store as he or she would have had experience in the trade. He or she may know where to buy at the best prices, offer the best advice and service and create a customer base, which will keep customers coming back.

10 One reason is that if the rival is successful, then there must be a market in that location for the business to tap into. Also, people often associate an area of a town with a type of product so they will deliberately shop there for that product. Hence it makes sense to set up there.

Chapter 5: **Added value**

1.   Jacob Simms is a solo singer who tours the country appearing at concerts and reviews.

     Select **one** answer.

     A   the total costs of putting on the concerts **minus** the revenue earned from selling tickets to his concerts

     B   what he makes in fees **minus** his costs such as petrol and hotels

     C   the total costs of the concerts at which he appears **minus** what he has to pay to the concert hall owners

     D   the wage he pays himself **minus** what he spends

     Answer B

Comments
A Incorrect – this will take value away.
B Correct – this is his only source of added value – the difference between his bought in costs and the money he earns from the concert.
C Incorrect – they are both forms of cost.
D Incorrect – this is a cost not a part of added value.

2.   Which **two** of the following might be a source of added value for a farming business?

     Select **two** answers.

     A   Quality of products grown on the farm

     B   The wages of the farm workers

     C   The profit earned by the farmer

     D   Speed of delivery from harvesting to the customer

     E   The receipts from sales of farm produce

     Answer A and D

Comments
A Correct – quality does add value to the product for both supplier and consumer and allows the farmer to charge higher prices.
B Incorrect – they are part of the costs of production.
C Incorrect – this is a result of added value not source.
D Correct – this is important to customers and makes the supplier more competitive.
E Incorrect – these are a record of sales not a source of added value.

3. Why is added value important to the survival of a business?

Select **one** answer.

It is important because:

A   added value allows a business to target its customers successfully

B   added value always means a better quality of product

C   a business that has negative value added is one that is not likely to be making enough money to pay its costs

D   all businesses have to have a unique selling point

Answer C

Comments
A Incorrect – added value does not necessarily mean that the business can target customers more effectively.
B Incorrect – quality does not always add value to a product.
C Correct – this is the added value measure for the business.
D Incorrect – it is not necessarily true that all businesses have a unique selling point.

Chapter 5: Added value

Corey Molnar was the manager of a garage. He had worked his way up through the trade, starting at 16 as an apprentice mechanic. Hard work and reliability had led to successive promotions. He had recently inherited a property. He felt that now was the right time to open his own garage business using the money from the sale of the house.

Within a few miles' radius of where he hoped to set up, there were garages for all the major brands of cars such as Ford, Citroen or Toyota. As official franchises of these companies, their mechanics were specially trained to work on these makes of cars. They also only used parts approved by the car manufacturer in services and repairs. Corey knew he had no hope of getting a franchise for a major car company. Instead, he would have to set up as an independent garage. This would keep down the cost of establishing a business anyway.

Competition from other independent garages would be tough. Corey planned to buy an existing garage rather than start the business from scratch. The garage would therefore come with an existing set of customers. However, he planned to expand and make the business more successful. Working as a manager, Corey knew that personal customers valued competitive prices, high quality workmanship and service feedback. The mechanics that did a job would be the ones who would report back to customers on the work done on a car. Corey also wanted to employ a female mechanic who would work on cars delivered by female customers. This could be a big selling point for the business amongst the growing number of female drivers who arranged their own repairs and servicing.

1. Explain **two** ways in which an official franchise garage for a company like Ford or Toyota adds value to the service it provides. (6)

Indicative content

- Quality - fully trained mechanics to set standards, official parts only/known quality.
- Known brand – reputation and track record.
- Convenience – likely to be located in many parts of the country as a national franchise.

Mark scheme

Two appropriate methods are identified (1 mark for each) along with some explanation of how it adds value to the service it provides. For example, 'An official franchise garage for a company like Ford or Toyota will have quality standards set by the franchise, (1 mark) including only using approved parts and employing fully trained staff. They must maintain these standards. (1 mark) Customers will know this and feel that it adds value to the service.' (1 mark)

2. Explain **two** unique selling points of Corey Molnar's new business? (6)

Indicative content

- Female mechanic
- Direct contact between mechanics and customers
- Mechanics cover all makes, not just the franchise
- Likely to be mechanics not just fitters / more experience

Mark scheme

Two appropriate USPs are identified (1 mark for each) along with explanation (maximum 2 marks for each). For example, 'A unique selling point of the business is that it has a female mechanic. (1 mark) There are likely to be relatively few female mechanics in the industry so this makes Corey's business different. (1 mark) They might draw female customers to the garage rather than to those of rivals, as females may feel more comfortable with a female mechanic. (1 mark)

3. Do you think that Corey Molnar will make a success of his garage business? Justify your answer.

(6)

Indicative content

Yes

- Has existing customer base
- Fills possible gaps in market – especially for female motorists
- Has worked hard and is reliable – two qualities of an entrepreneur
- Recognises customer needs
- Knows his market so has targeted the added values
- Has USP
- Has good start up capital – reduces some fixed costs.

No

- Competition is tough from existing franchises
- May have image issue, good or bad, from previous business
- Do not know what competitors are offering

Mark scheme

Level	Mark	Descriptor
	No mark	Non-rewardable material
Level 1	1–2	A choice will be made with poorly developed justification and supported by limited examples. For example, 'Yes, because the business has a number of unique selling points.'
Level 2	3–4	A choice will be made with some developed justification and supported by some good examples. For example, 'Yes. The business has a number of unique selling points such as the female mechanic, competitive prices, high quality workmanship and good feedback. These add value to a business if competitors do not have them. This is attractive to customers and could give Corey an advantage over franchises.'
Level 3	5–6	A choice will be made with a clearly developed justification supported by excellent examples. Answers in this range will tend to have some balance. For example, 'Corey may find that competition is tough from national franchises, which have a known brand and a good reputation. But he has a number of unique selling points which can attract customers, such as a female mechanic. He may also be able to offer more competitive prices and personal service for customers. This personal service may be a USP which larger franchises do not offer in the same way and so, together with the other qualities, this has led to his business being a success.'

Chapter 5: **Added value**

1   What is meant by the term 'USP'?

2   What is meant by the term 'bought in costs'?

3   What is meant by the term 'added value'?

4   Why is added value important for a business?

5   A business pays £1.27 for materials to make a product. It sells the product for £3.45. What is the value added?

6   State two features of the design of a computer that might add value.

7   Explain how a brand allows a business to add value.

8   What might be a USP of a female tiler advertising herself as 'Bonnie Tiler'?

9   A product costs a manufacturer £2.00 to produce. The manufacturer sells the product to the retailer for £2.80. The retailer sells it to customers for £3.99. Which business has added the most value (in pounds)?

10 Why can some shops sell the latest games console with such a high 'added value'?

Suggested answers

1   A USP is a Unique Selling Point. This is the characteristic that differentiates one product completely from another.

2   Bought in costs are costs that are bought by the business from outside suppliers to assist in production, e.g. raw materials and gas for heating.

3   Added value is the increased worth that a business creates for a product.

4   Added value is the difference between what the business pays and the price it is able to charge for its product. If a business adds value to its products it charges a higher price than it pays. This will help a business to survive, be successful and make a profit.

5   Value added is £3.45 - 1.27 = £2.18.

6   Examples might include size of hard drive, speed of operation, portability and size of screen.

7   Customers are willing to pay more for branded product. People differentiate branded products from other products and often see them as being of superior quality. The brand reflects the way they want to present themselves and they are willing to pay extra for this.

8   The fact that she is female. This might encourage other women to employ her as they might feel safer with her and believe that she would show would more empathy.

9   The manufacturer adds value of 80p (£2.80 - £2.00). The retailer adds on £1.19 (£2.80 - £3.99). So the retailer adds the most value.

10 When a new games console comes out there is an image of 'must have'. There is scarcity at first and it is likely the product itself will have unique technology. These create a USP for the product. This creates a situation where customers feel there is a USP in being the first to have the new product. All these factors lead to high added value.

Chapter 6: Franchising

1. Which **one** of the following is a correct statement about **franchisees**?

    Select **one** answer.

    A   Franchisees sell the right to make a product to franchisors

    B   Franchisees receives a royalty from franchisors

    C   Franchisees receive training and support from franchisors

    D   Franchisees sell materials for use in production to franchisors

    Answer C

Comments
A Incorrect – it is the other way around - franchisors sell the right to make a product to franchisees.
B Incorrect – it is the other way around – franchisors receive a royalty from franchisees.
C Correct – these are possible reasons for buying a franchise.
D Incorrect – suppliers sell these, not franchisees.

2. Which **two** of the following are most likely to be advantages of taking on a franchise rather than setting up as a sole trader or private limited company?

    Select **two** answers.

    A   The franchisor provides a tried and tested product to sell

    B   The franchisor pays the franchisee to set up in business

    C   The franchisee receives ongoing help and support from the franchisor

    D   The franchisor is responsible for paying the taxes of the business

    E   Franchisees do not need to have so many business skills as people who set up on their own

    Answer A and C

Comments
A Correct – it is likely to already be an established business.
B Incorrect – it is the other way around.
C Correct – these are two key benefits of taking on a franchise.
D Incorrect – the franchisee is responsible for their own tax liabilities.
E Incorrect – they are still setting up and running their own business so still need lots of skills.

3. Which **two** of the following are most likely to be **disadvantages** of becoming a franchisee rather than setting up your own business?

Select **two** answers.

A   Franchises are more likely to fail than businesses which have been set up independently

B   The franchisee has to pay a fee to the franchisor for setting up in business

C   Franchises tend to sell products that are unpopular with customers

D   The franchisee cannot sell the business without the franchisor's permission

E   Franchisees need far more business skills to be successful than people who set up on their own

Answer B and D

Comments
A Incorrect – the product is tried and tested so less likely to fail.
B Correct – it is a cost which someone setting up their own business, independently, does not have to pay.
C Incorrect – the whole idea of a franchise is that the product is popular.
D Correct – the person who owns their own business can sell it at any time and to anybody.
E Incorrect – the same business skills are needed regardless of the nature of the business.

Chapter 6: Franchising

Merry Maids – domestic cleaning services

Merry Maids is a franchise that provides domestic cleaning services for households.

Merry Maids are looking for mature couples or individuals to acquire ownership of a Merry Maids Franchise who have the skills to manage a fast growing business and the cleaning staff who work within it.

Merry Maids specialised, two person cleaning concept and accompanying pay incentives attract people who seek part time weekday employment, convenient hours and above average salaries on the quality and quantity of the homes they service. These employees are among Merry Maid's greatest assets, hence the initial franchise fee charged by Merry Maid also includes an exclusive and unique service worker selection program to make sure you bring the right people into your business.

Also included in the initial franchise fee is the equipment, supplies and exclusive Merry Maids' cleaning products to equip four two person cleaning teams. Each cleaning team, when properly trained and scheduled, can clean two to three homes a day.

Merry Maids exclusive Business Management System is yet another important factor that has attributed to the company's position of Market Leader.

Franchise Fee: £9,950 (Plus VAT)

Equipment Package: £5,700 (Plus VAT)

Royalty fee: 7%

TruGreen

TruGreen is a franchise opportunity that allows enterprising individuals to enter the profitable and growing lawn care market and provide specialist services on the highest of levels. The franchise benefits from the respected professional standing of its parent company, ServiceMaster limited. It operates with low overheads and attractive margins and is an enjoyable and potentially rewarding business.

TruGreen offers a franchise that means:

• You can work from home, with low overheads, plus great Monday to Friday daytime hours.

• Your franchise will be in the service sector with exceptional growth predictions.

• No cash flow problems and high profit margins.

• 90% repeat customers, in your own territory.

Franchise Fee: £15,000 (Plus VAT)

Equipment Package: £10,500

Royalty fee: 10%

Source: adapted from www.franchise-uk.co.uk

ServiceMaster is a successful US franchisor which came to Britain in 1959. Today it has over 900 franchisees in the UK covering 6 different businesses. Two of these are Merry Maids and TruGreen.

Jim and Dot Truepenny are looking to operate a franchise. Jim is 52 and has just been made redundant from his job as a maintenance supervisor, responsible amongst other things for health and safety. Dot works in a garden shop. They are both keen gardeners. Jim was given a redundancy package which included a payment of £22,500.

BUSINESS

1. Identify the services being offered by Merry Maids and TruGreen. (6)

Indicative content
- Merry Maids – Domestic/home cleaning services.
- TruGreen – Lawn care.

Mark scheme
I mark for each service.

2. How much would it cost, in total, for Jim and Dot to set up (a) a Merry Maids franchise (2) and (b) a TruGreen franchise? (2)

(a) Merry Maids:
Franchise fee = £9,950 plus VAT @17.5% + Equipment package = £5,700 plus VAT @17.5%

= £9,950 + £1,741.25 + £5,700 + £997.50

= £11,691.25 + £6,697.50

= £18,388,75   (2 marks)

(b) TruGreen
Franchise fee = £15,000 plus VAT @ 17.5% + Equipment package = £10,500

= £15,000 + £2,625 + £10,500

= £28,125   (2 marks)

* Note – at standard VAT rates of 17.5%

3. Explain **one** advantage and **one** disadvantage to Jim and Dot of setting up in business as a franchisee rather than setting up an independent business. (6)

Indicative content

Advantages
- Brand/ reputation
- Training
- Equipment
- Assistance in selection
- Exclusive area

Disadvantages
- Initial cost
- Royalty payments
- Lack of flexibility/ scope on services
- May be hard to sell on
- Could have franchise withdrawn

Mark scheme

One appropriate advantage is identified and one appropriate disadvantage is identified (1 mark for each) along with an appropriate explanation (maximum 2 marks for each). For example, 'One advantage of setting up as franchise is that the franchise has an existing reputation. (1 mark) Starting a new business can be a problem as it takes time to build up brand loyalty. (1 mark) Using the brand name of an existing well known company can attract customers quickly, helping a business to avoid problems of lack of cash associated with some star-ups.' (1 mark)

4.   Which of the two franchises do you think would most suit Jim and Dot? Justify your answer.   (6)

Indicative content

- Management service provided by MM.
- Both have gardening skills – needed for TG.
- Can afford MM franchise outright (redundancy money).
- No evidence they know the domestic cleaning market.
- MM leave them with some cash spare.
- Can just 'run' MM not 'work' it. Dot can keep her job.
- TG has higher royalty payment and higher set up cost.

Mark scheme

Level	Mark	Descriptor
	No mark	Non-rewardable material
Level 1	1–2	A choice will be made with poorly developed justification and supported by limited examples. For example, 'Jim and Dot should choose the TruGreen franchise as they have gardening skills.'
Level 2	3–4	A choice will be made with some developed justification and supported by some good examples. For example, 'Jim and Dot should choose the Merry Maids franchise. They can afford to pay for the set up fee of £18,388,75 from their redundancy money (£22,500) without any further borrowing. Merry Maids also provides equipment and staff recruitment, which can help a new business to be successful.'
Level 3	5–6	A choice will be made with a clearly developed justification and supported by excellent examples. For example, 'Jim and Dot might consider choosing the Merry Maids franchise. They can afford to pay for the set up fee (£18,388,75) from their redundancy money (£22,500) and still have some funds left over. To pay for a TruGreen Franchise (£28,125) they may need to borrow. However, they are keen gardeners and have the skills to make this a success. They have no experience of the cleaning market. With this knowledge and experience they should choose TruGreen. Even though costs are higher they are more likely to make a successful business because they know more about the service they will be selling.'

Chapter 6: **Franchising**

1   What is meant by the term 'franchise'?

2   What is meant by the term 'franchisee'?

3   What is meant by the term 'franchisor'?

4   State four benefits of buying a franchise.

5   State four drawbacks of buying a franchise.

6   What is meant by the term 'royalty fee'?

7   What problem would you face if you got fed up with running your franchise and wanted to sell it?

8   State four disadvantages of buying a franchised milk round.

9   Explain why operating in a unique area can help a new business franchise.

10 Explain two advantages of operating a franchise in a department store.

Suggested answers

1 A franchise is a legal agreement or right, given by one business to another (or to a person) to sell its goods or services using the original business' name, e.g. McDonald's.

2 A franchisee is the person buying the franchise.

3 The franchisor is the original business selling the franchise.

4 Benefits are a known product/ brand, the provision of training and support, products/equipment provided, advertising paid for, unique location, R & D by parent company and a 'formula' for success.

5 Drawbacks are having to pay a fee up front, paying royalties, that it may be hard to sell on, that the business can lose the franchise without warning and that the franchisee is never independent.

6 Where the franchisee pays either a percentage of the turnover that she or he makes to the franchisor to continue to operate a franchise or pays a set monthly fee to 'use' the franchise.

7 You could not sell the franchise without the permission of the franchisor as the franchisor always owns the franchise.

8 Disadvantages include that demand for this type of service is falling as more people buy from supermarkets, that milk delivered can be more expensive than at the supermarket, that the franchisee never owns the business so he or she cannot just 'get out', that the franchisee may have to work unsocial hours and that the franchisee cannot afford to be ill if they operate on their own.

9 Setting up a new business is always difficult, especially if there is competition which offers similar products in the nearby area. Operating as a franchisee means that no other business in the franchise is allowed to set up too close. This gives the new business a market to target for customers with no other business with similar brand or similar advantages close by. Having less competition may help it to attract customers and make a profit.

10 One advantage of opening a franchise in a department store is that the franchisee is saved many costs. For example, heating and lighting are paid for by the store, which will then share it between the franchises, thus cutting the cost to one franchise. Customers will be coming into the store, so the franchisee will benefit from that. They will also benefit from the store's reputation so there will be less need to pay for advertising.

Practice exam questions

> Dara Coyle was an excellent cook. She was also keen on growing organic food. Dara often went to garden centres and noticed that many of them had cafés. Although the aroma of the cafés was enticing Dara thought the food was often overpriced and nothing special. She thought she could do better. The idea occurred to her to open up her own business, selling homemade food using home grown products.
>
> Dara decided to do some research and she observed the buying habits of customers at several garden centre cafes. This convinced her there were different groups of buyers and that she could meet the needs of some of them. Dara tried out her menus on some local people who told her they were delighted with the high quality taste of the food, the fact it was local and that they could talk with the 'boss'. Encouraged by this Dara started trading as 'Goodness Nose.' Dara knew that she would face competition from the garden centres and maybe other cafés. However, her research had convinced her that the quality of her products set her apart from the rest, that they would sell and she would make a profit. They might be bigger and cheaper but her products were truly local.

(a) **Two** Unique Selling Points for a product or service could be the:

A image of the product
B place to put a price label
C somewhere to advertise
D design of the product
E amount of points the buyer earns on their loyalty card
F strength of the competition

Answer A and D

Examiner's comment
A Correct – many products sell on image more than anything else; what people think they are.
B Incorrect – this might not be unique to any one business.
C Incorrect – the place of advertising is not unique.
D Correct – one-off designs or original designs make the product/ service unique.
E Incorrect – the amount of points does not make it unique.
F Incorrect – it is irrelevant. A USP would help a business overcome this competition.

(b) (i) Identify one way Dara can add value to her products. (4)

(ii) Explain how this way will help Dara to add value to her products. (3)

Indicative content

(i) Possible ways include the following:

- Providing high quality food.
- Excellent service for customers.
- The fact that the food is 100% organic.
- The food is entirely homemade.
- Service is highly personal.
- The range of food she provides.
- The convenience with which customers can access her products – the speed and efficiency of service for example.
- Providing a special service for those with disabilities – reserved areas, waitress service, brail menus etc.

Mark scheme

(ii) Do not give a mark for the repetition of the reason.

For 1 mark, with the explanation will be limited. For example, 'Organic food is something that people now go for'.

For 2–3 marks the explanation offers more links, for example 'Excellent service is something that customers are prepared to pay for' (1 mark). The quality of the service is something that could set her business apart. (1 mark) Customers will feel their experience with the business is of high quality and won't mind paying for such good service. (1 mark)

(c) Dara has plans to expand her business through offering it as a franchise if it is a success. In your opinion, would this type of business make a suitable franchise? Justify your answer. *(6)*

Indicative content

Considerations

- Very personal
- Local product
- Relies of her skills
- Level of competition
- Product may be difficult to replicate
- USP might not work elsewhere
- Target market
- Location
- Is there anything to buy?
- Branding or lack of
- Training
- Advertising
- Sole trader

Mark scheme

Level	Mark	Descriptor
	No mark	Non-rewardable material
Level 1	1–2	A limited attempt is made to justify a decision, for example, 'This business would not make a suitable franchise because it is too specific.' Alternatively, 'This business would make a suitable franchise because it does not need much money to set up.'
Level 2	3–4	A decision is made with some justification, for example, 'This business would not make a suitable franchise. The product made is based on Dara's skills, which could be difficult to replicate elsewhere'. 'This business would not make a suitable franchise. It has strong USP, using home grown products. This could create a brand which can be used be used to sell the product.'
Level 3	5–6	The evaluation would be considered, with advantages and disadvantages examined. There will be sequential comments. For example, 'This business would not make a suitable franchise. There is a strong USP, using home grown products. However, it is a very local product, which means it relies on local skills and produce on demand. These might not be available elsewhere, so it may not be easy to replicate. The business also relies heavily on Dara's skills which others may not have.' Alternatively, 'This business would make a franchise. It has a strong USP, using home grown products. But it relies on Dara's kills. So it might only be successful in a very specific target market and for businesses buying into the franchise and Dara would need to be certain about the brand or she would have to provide excellent training and be careful who she awards the franchise to.'

Case study

Antawan Hayes is a keen cycle rider, but finds that punctures happen too often and always at an inconvenient moment. Antawan is also a keen inventor and entrepreneur. Sometimes, his inventions come from accidental creativity, when he chances upon a discovery. Other times, inventions come from deliberate creativity, when he spends a great deal of time working through a problem. With inventions, lateral thinking is needed. Antawan, like many inventors, finds he has to think of the unusual and unexpected to come up with a solution to a problem.

Last year, Antawan decided to tackle the problem of bicycle tyre punctures. He began to work on the idea of injecting a substance into the tyre, which would automatically find the hole, cover it with a layer of material and repair the puncture. He kept asking himself questions such as 'What?', 'Why?' and 'What if?' He needed to look beyond the obvious.

If he could crack the technical problem, Antawan knew there was a long road ahead of him to get the product to market. An invention protected by a patent was one thing. Successful innovation was another. Planning, thinking ahead, seeing business opportunities and drive and determination were enterprise skills he would need. He also knew that the probability of success was low. There were so many risks that he faced. He thought that he stood a less than 1 in 100 chance of getting an invention stocked in bicycle shops. However, Antawan was not afraid to take risks and was always willing to undertake new ventures.

Having worked on the problem for six months, Antawan could find no satisfactory solution. He weighed up the risks and rewards of continuing to work on the idea and decided that his idea was probably not viable. So he abandoned the work and began searching round for a new idea.

Suggested discussion points/answers

1. Explain whether (a) a bicycle and (b) a bicycle repair at a bicycle repair shop are goods or services.

(a) Good
- Physical product
- Can be handled and used

(b) Service
- Non-physical
- Making right
- Fixing
- As new
- Specialised skill

2. What enterprise skills does an entrepreneur like Antawan need?
- Creativity
- Drive and determination
- Planning
- Risk taker
- Belief
- Judgement
- Thinking ahead

3. (a) What is the difference between invention and innovation and (b) why are both important for Antawan's puncture repair idea?

(a)
- Invention – design and create
- Innovation – getting it into a format that is usable
- and getting it to the market

(b)
- 2 stage operation
- Invention then innovation
- Invention exists but useless without innovation
- No invention, no innovation

4. Do you think that having a 'less than 1 in 100 chance of getting a successful invention stocked in bicycle shops' means that Antawan should never have spent any time trying to develop his invention? Justify your answer.

No

- Little chance of success

- Could waste time

- Could cost him money

- Could be doing other things which could be more successful

Yes

- Odds might be wrong

- Someone has to be the 1%

- May have found another product by accident

- Got him thinking

- Raised awareness

- Made him determined to succeed

- Learned from mistakes

- Needed to see it end naturally

Chapter 7: **What is enterprise?**

1. Which **three** of the following are most likely to be examples of being enterprising?

    Select **three** answers.

    A   Being made redundant

    B   Carrying out an order from your boss

    C   Taking risks

    D   Taking the initiative

    E   Taking your summer holiday at a time convenient for your employer

    F   Undertaking a new venture

    G   Being told that your job with change

    Answer C, D and F

Comments
A Incorrect – it is about losing a job and is not related to enterprise.
B Incorrect – it is about doing only what you're told rather than taking the initiative.
C Correct – enterprise involves a step into the unknown so there is a risk.
D Correct – being enterprising needs you to take the idea forward yourself.
E Incorrect – it is not relevant at all
F Correct – a new venture needs enterprise to get it going.
G Incorrect – that is a decision made by others.

2. Which **three** of the following are examples of services?

    Select **three** of the following.

    A   A school desk

    B   A train carriage

    C   A tonne of coal

    D   A knife and fork

    E   Menus advice in a restaurant

    F   Education in a state school

    Answer D, F and G

Comments
A Incorrect – it is a good, it is physical.
B Incorrect – it is a good, it is physical.
C Incorrect – it is a good, it is physical.
D Correct – it is non-physical and is a facility supplied.
E Incorrect – they are physical goods.
F Correct – it is non-physical and is a facility supplied.
G Correct – it is non-physical and is a facility supplied.

3. Lewis Hunting runs a hairdressers. Which **one** of the following is correct?

    Select **one** answer.

    A   A haircut is an example of a service.

    B   There are no risks in running a hairdressing business.

    C   A bottle of shampoo is an example of a service.

    D   Lewis Hunting never needs to show initiative in running his business.

    Answer A

Comments
A Correct – it is non-physical and there is no physical product made.
B Incorrect – there is a risk involved in operating any business.
C Incorrect – it is a good, a physical product.
D Incorrect – it is highly unlikely that Lewis would never need to show initiative to run his business.

Chapter 7: **What is enterprise?**

Charlotte Yelland had always loved horses. As a child, she had done lots of riding and spent as much time as possible at the stables where she kept the horse her parents had bought for her. As an adult, Charlotte had continued to ride even though she could no longer afford to keep a horse of her own.

Her break came when she inherited over half a million pounds. A local stables was up for sale and Charlotte decided to buy it. The stables were not making much money and so it was a risky venture for Charlotte. However, she thought she could turn the business round and establish a successful enterprise.

In her business plan, Charlotte outlined how she would transform the business. Currently, the main source of income was individual horse owners paying to have their horses kept at the stables. Charlotte wanted to open a riding school, offering riding lessons particularly to children. She also wanted to open a shop selling everything a horse rider might need such as saddles and riding hats. The business would be built up gradually over a five year period to reduce the risk of failure. Charlotte had been advised that very quick expansions often failed. Money to fund the expansion often ran out. Also, the owner could find themselves out of their depth too quickly, without enough time to sort out all the inevitable problems that come with an expanding business. Charlotte, though, hoped that she could build up the business more quickly than the years proposed in her business plan.

1. Explain why a horse riding hat is an example of a good, but a lesson at a horse riding school is an example of a service. (6)

Indicative content

- Physical product
- Something that is made
- Non-physical
- Facility
- Something that can be used by several people at one time
- Something which can be held
- Something which supports or develops a skill

Mark scheme

A suitable definition of a good (1 mark) and service (1 mark) is given. Up to 2 marks are then given for the explanation of why a hat is a good and up to 2 marks for why a riding lesson is a service.

2. Explain **three** different ways in which Charlotte is showing enterprise. (9)

Indicative content

a) **Opportunity**

- Stables available
- Already established so some reputation to use
- Market already exists so demand is known

b) **Risk**

- Currently losing money so has a risk element
- Minimising risk by careful planning
- Spreading risk by offering goods and services
- Knows the market
- Created a business plan to check viability and progress

c) **Initiative**

- Changing what is offered
- Keeping what is good, adapting what is not.
- Making use of money available
- Using her knowledge to good effect

Mark scheme

One mark each (up to a maximum of 3 marks) for identifying three appropriate ways in which Charlotte is showing enterprise. For each way, up to 2 marks for the explanation of how Charlotte is being entrepreneurial. For example, 'Charlotte took a risk. (1 mark) When she bought the stables they were not making much money. There was a risk that no matter what Charlotte did, they could have been unprofitable. (1 mark) She took a chance that they could be turned around with careful planning and slow development over five years.' (1 mark)

3. Would it be better if she expanded her business much more quickly than the five years she has put in her business plan? Justify your answer. (6)

Indicative content

No

- No external funding so no interest being paid on loans
- Not overstretching
- Easier to expand if going well than to contract
- Caution to minimise risks
- Advised to go slowly

Yes

- Shows drive and determination to back her hunch
- Captures the market/reduces scope of competition
- Provides both goods and services so all-in-one is a USP
- Demonstrates belief and willingness to take risk as an entrepreneur

Mark scheme

Level	Mark	Descriptor
	No mark	Non-rewardable material
Level 1	1–2	A choice will be made with poorly developed justification and supported by limited examples. For example, 'No. This is the period that planning had shown would make the business successful.' For example, 'No, because there is never a guarantee of success in business.'
Level 2	3–4	A choice will be made with some developed justification and supported by some good examples. For example, 'No. Although a shorter period would earn money more quickly, the plan had shown that it would take five years for the business to be successful. Charlotte took advice and found that businesses expanding more quickly often ran out of money.'
Level 3	5–6	A choice will be made with a clearly developed justification and supported by excellent examples. For example, 'Charlotte might consider expanding the business more quickly than five years. She has a large amount of money behind her and has identified a target market that could make the business successful. However, advice has shown that more rapid expansion can cause cash flow problems. So in conclusion Charlotte would be better following the carefully drafted business plan which indicates success would be less risky over a five year period.'

Chapter 7: **What is enterprise?**

1 What is meant by the term 'entrepreneur'?

2 What is meant by the term 'enterprise'?

3 What is the difference between goods and services?

4 List four examples of goods and four examples of services.

5 Explain why newspapers are a good but newspaper delivery is a service.

6 What is meant by the term 'initiative'?

7 Wasim set up a DVD and games console rental service after he noticed there was no shop within 10 miles of the town in which he lives that provided this service. Why did he show initiative?

8 What is meant by 'taking a risk'?

9 State three risks that might be involved in setting up a car valeting business.

10 Explain two reasons why setting up as a window cleaner may be wiser for a first time entrepreneur than buying and selling houses.

Suggested answers

1 Someone who is prepared to take on the risks of setting up and running his or her own business.

2 The willingness to take risks, show initiative and undertake new ventures.

3 Goods are physical products whilst services are non-physical.

4 Examples of goods could be mobile phones, handbags, jewellery, football boots and perfume.

 Examples of services could be a taxi ride, window cleaning, hair styling, manicures, banking, gardening and accountancy.

5 Newspapers are physical products so they are goods. The delivery of newspapers is a non-physical product, so it is a service.

6 Taking control of the destiny of a situation and being the first to make things happen rather than sitting back and waiting to see what happens.

7 Wasim showed initiative as he saw there was a gap in the market and did something about this. He was the first to offer this service in his area.

8 Understanding the possible loss that could occur through setting up a business, but deciding it is worthwhile setting up anyway.

9 Risks might include that there are not enough customers, that there is a need for high investment in machinery that might be hard to sell on, that competition may force down prices and profits and that recession may lead to people valeting cars themselves.

10 One reason is that less may need to be put into the business at first. Cash flow could be better as people pay for this service as it happens. Also, if a window cleaner loses one customer, it will have less effect on the business than if one house sale falls through.

Chapter 8: **Thinking creatively**

1. Jacob attends a course on setting up a business. On the course, he participates in a blue skies thinking session. Which **one** of the following is most likely to be correct?

   Select **one** answer.

   Blue skies thinking

   A   will put him at a competitive disadvantage when he starts his own business

   B   is an example of creative thinking

   C   is the opposite of lateral thinking

   D   discourages people from thinking of new ideas

   Answer B

Comments
A Incorrect – it should put him at an advantage.
B Correct – it is about random ideas which might lead to a feasible one.
C Incorrect – blue skies thinking is very similar to lateral thinking.
D Incorrect – blue skies thinking is the opposite and encourages people to think of new ideas.

2. Alfie Tarrach is setting up a sandwich making business. Which **one** of the following is most likely to give his business a competitive advantage?

   Select **one** answer.

   A   High quality locally sourced ingredients

   B   High borrowing costs

   C   Shorter opening hours than competitors

   D   Expensive rent on his premises

   Answer A

Comments
A Correct – this may set his business apart from others. Could be his USP.
B Incorrect – this may give him a competitive disadvantage.
C Incorrect – this would cause a disadvantage.
D Incorrect – this would not give him an advantage.

3. Courtney Farnham is investigating setting up in business as a dance teacher and is thinking particularly of how she could attract pupils to take up her dance classes. Which **one** of the following is most likely for her to be an example of lateral thinking about attracting customers?

Select **one** answer.

A   She will have to give up her present job with a salary of £20,000 a year.

B   It would be a good idea for her to take out insurance in case of accidents to her pupils.

C   She should get advice from experts on how to set up a business.

D   She could give singing lessons for pupils that wanted to perform in musicals.

Answer D

Comments
A Incorrect – it has nothing to do with the new business.
B Incorrect – that would be part of her business plan.
C Incorrect – that would come when she had decided to go ahead.
D Correct – she is thinking creatively and finding different ways to exploit her business opportunities.

Chapter 8: **Thinking creatively**

Lily Ashbourne is at university studying Graphic Design. She is in her final year and thinking about her future. Ideally, she would like to set up her own business and has come up with the idea of designing greetings cards, such as birthday cards and wedding cards, and cards that can be included with presents.

She has already used blue skies thinking to consider possible options. For example, would it be best to get a job with an established card company? Would it be possible to design cards but get them printed by someone else? Should she print them herself? What about having unique hand painted cards that would be sold at a high price? How is she going to get her cards to customers? Would it be best to sell them to shops or set up a shop herself to sell her own designs?

Gaining a competitive advantage would be essential if she were to be successful. How could she establish a competitive advantage? One of her careers advisors suggested she should go on a course about setting up in business. Whilst on the course, she was taught to use the Six Thinking Hats technique. When she put on the Red Hat, she felt passionately committed to the idea of making greetings cards. However, putting on the Black Hat made her realise just how many obstacles there were in the way of setting up in business successfully. However, she was convinced that, by using techniques which stimulated creative thinking, she could overcome these problems.

1. Explain, using Lily Ashbourne's case, what is meant by 'blue skies thinking'. (3)

Indicative content

- Creative thinking
- Different approaches to the same topic (selling cards)
- The different options open to her.

Mark scheme

A suitable definition of blue skies thinking is given (1 mark), for example 'a technique of creative thinking which encourages people to think of as many ideas as possible about an issue or a problem'. Up to 2 marks for the explanation of how Lily used blue skies thinking. For example 'Lily had to consider what would be the important features of her business and so would have to think of as many options as possible (1 mark). She considered all aspects of this, including the type of product, the price, the way they are sold and how they would be made.' (1 mark).

2. Explain, using Lily Ashbourne's case, what is meant by 'lateral thinking'. (3)

Indicative content

- Thinking outside the box
- Thinking differently
- Considering alternative approaches and uses for cards that may not exist at present
- Looking for gaps in the market.

Mark scheme

A suitable definition of lateral thinking is given (1 mark), for example 'thinking differently to try and find new and unexpected ideas'. Up to 2 marks for the explanation of how Lily used lateral thinking. For example, 'Lily used the Six Thinking Hats process to consider her position. This is an example of lateral thinking. (1 mark) It forced her to consider different ways about how she felt about the business idea, using the Red Hat, and the potential problems, using the Black Hat'. (1 mark)

3. Lily could sell cards herself or sell them through shops. Which do you think would be best for Lily? Justify your answer. (6)

Indicative content

Through shops

- Dedicated market
- Reputation
- Expertise
- Shift responsibility
- Guaranteed customers
- She has no knowledge in this area

Herself

- Keeps all the profit
- Has control of pricing/merchandising
- Build up customer base
- Interaction with customers
- Gain knowledge about customer needs/can react and change if needed

Mark scheme

Level	Mark	Descriptor
	No mark	Non-rewardable material
Level 1	1–2	A choice will be made with poorly developed justification and supported by limited examples. For example, 'Sell them through a shop as she lacks experience.'
Level 2	3–4	A choice will be made with some developed justification and supported by some good examples. For example, 'Lily might want to sell them herself to retain control, but selling through a shop could reduce risk. She lacks experience and shops will be able to reach a large market so this would be a better option.'
Level 3	5–6	A choice will be made with a clearly developed justification, the answer has some balance and is supported by excellent examples. For example, 'Lily may have a strong wish to sell cards herself. She will have more control over the business and may be able to keep control of her costs. If she produces a specialised product, such as had painted cards, she may feel in a better position to target the market. However, she has no experience of selling and the card market is very competitive. So even though she may lose some control, selling through established retail outlets might give her a greater chance of success.'

4. Do you think that Lily Ashbourne could gain a competitive advantage over the major producers of greetings cards in the UK? Justify your answer. (9)

Indicative content

Yes

- Individuality
- Enthusiasm
- Belief
- Fresh/in touch with modern thinking
- Drive and determination
- Location may help/USP in area

No

- Lack of business expertise
- No reputation
- Lack of awareness of competition
- Financial constraints/ cash flow
- Market might be flooded already
- Ability to advertise
- Distribution

Mark scheme

Level	Mark	Descriptor
	No mark	Non-rewardable material
Level 1	1–3	A choice will be made with limited justification and supported by limited examples. For example, 'Yes. She has a unique product. This could appeal to people who wan to buy different cards.'
Level 2	4–6	A choice will be made with some developed justification and supported by some good examples. 'Yes. Although she has limited experience and no reputation, she has a unique product. This could appeal to sections of the market who want to buy different and original cards. Hand painted products would have a USP, therefore, which could stand out.'
Level 3	7–9	A choice will be made with a clearly developed justification and balance, supported by excellent examples. For example, 'It could be difficult for Lily to establish a competitive advantage over rivals. The market for cards is very competitive. She has limited experience and, as a new business, will have to establish a loyal market. However, there are aspects of her product that could appeal to customers. Hand painted cards could be seen as a premium product and she could charge a relatively high price. They may be seen as unique and different to other cards. So she may be able to establish some competitive advantage in a limited target market.'

Chapter 8: Thinking creatively

1   What is meant by the term 'deliberate creativity'?

2   What is meant by the term 'lateral thinking'?

3   Natalie found that leaflets advertising her pottery business did not bring in much business so she contacted local cafes to suggest that she could provide them with free bowls, cups and plates if they would tell people about her business. Why might this be an example of lateral thinking?

4   What is a meant by the term 'blue skies thinking'?

5   List five features that might be written down when using blue skies thinking about a new style of jeans.

6   List the Six Thinking Hats.

7   Colm wants to set up a children's party business in a seaside town where there are lots of older people. How could black hat thinking help him?

8   What is meant by the term 'competitive advantage'?

9   State four ways in which a restaurant business could have a competitive advantage over a competitor.

10 State two features of a village shop that might give it a competitive advantage over a national supermarket located on an out of town trading estate.

Suggested answers

1 Deliberate creativity is where someone, or a team of people, sets out with a plan to improve on a situation and looks at where some elements of what currently exists can be improved, by using tested structured methods of 'thinking'.

2 This is 'thinking outside the box' and means looking at something in a different way in order to find a solution.

3 Lateral thinking is 'thinking outside the box' and looking for ideas that have not previously been considered. Natalie's use of cafes to advertise her business is an example of thinking differently and one which may not have been considered by others before.

4 Blue skies thinking is a way of thinking where someone, or a team of people, write down as many random ideas as possible surrounding a problem to see if a solution emerges.

5 Examples might be blue, colour, denim, colour, shape, cut, ripped, pockets, waist sizes, pictures, branding, price, zip.

6 White (Facts), Yellow (Positive), Green (Creative), Red (Gut feeling), Blue (Reasoning), Black (Difficulties).

7 Black hat thinking is about the problems or difficulties of an idea. A problem for Colm is that there may not be enough children in the area for the idea to work.

8 Competitive advantage is something that a business does to get ahead of its rivals and something it can continue to develop, sustain and use to maintain that advantage. It is an advantage that others cannot easily copy and which is distinct to the business.

9 Examples include lower costs, type of food, location and service.

10 One feature is that there is less distance to travel to get to the supermarket and less time is wasted. Another is that people who do not have a car or do not want the cost of transport can use it.

Chapter 9: Questions to be asked

1. Ethan Blake is developing a new product for the market. It is a software program that will allow a user instantly to compare different results from different search engines on the Internet. Which **one** of the following questions should he ask himself if he wants to find out whether there will be customers for his product?

   Select **one** answer.

   A   How many programs will I sell if I charge £20 per copy?

   B   What will be the costs of production?

   C   How much should I spend on advertising?

   D   Where might customers want their orders delivered?

   Answer A

Comments
A Correct – this will tell him if the market exists.
B Incorrect – the cost has nothing to do with customer demand.
C Incorrect – this is part of his marketing mix not demand.
D Incorrect – they will tell him and it comes after demand has been met.

2. Callum Fisher has decided to set up a shop selling teenage fashion clothes. He is worried about whether the business will be financially successful. Which **one** of the following questions is the **most** important to ask himself if he wants to research this more fully?

   Select **one** answer.

   A   What if I spend my money on going on holiday to Turkey rather than to Spain?

   B   What if the bank charges a very high rate of interest on the money I will borrow?

   C   What if I have to get up half an hour earlier to get to work on time?

   D   What if I get 10 applications for the job of sales assistant in the shop?

   Answer B

Comments
A Incorrect – it's about his social life not the business.
B Correct – this is a cost and will affect his cash flow negatively.
C Incorrect – it has nothing to do with finance.
D Incorrect – this is about recruitment not finance.

3. Connor Reely is thinking of setting up a restaurant. He wants his restaurant to offer customers something different from other restaurants in his local area. Which **one** of the following questions is he likely to ask himself when researching this difference?

Select **one** answer.

A   Why not get a bank loan?

B   Why not do the laundry on the premises rather than sending it out to professional cleaners?

C   Why not buy an estate car rather than a van for the business?

D   Why not offer 100% organic food on the menu?

Answer D

Comments
A Incorrect – the bank loan has nothing to do with research.
B Incorrect – this is about running the business not what it offers.
C Incorrect – this has nothing to do with being different.
D Correct – other restaurants may not be offering this.

Chapter 9: **Questions to be asked**

Ling Tan is thinking of setting up a business producing luxury leather wedding albums. The albums would be sold mainly to professional wedding photographers, who in turn would sell them to their clients.

The production of the albums is a highly specialised, skilled task. The outside of the wedding album is made of the finest leather. Ling Tan intends initially to do this work herself. As the business becomes more established and orders rise, she hopes to be able to hire and train up another worker to share in the production work.

Her business premises at the start will be her double garage. However, she expects to have to rent larger premises if the business becomes established and successful.

1. (a) Suggest **one** question that Ling Tan should be asking at this stage about her possible customers. (3)

    (b) Explain why she should ask this question. (3)

Indicative content

(a)

- What type of product do customers want to buy?
- How many customers might there be?
- Where are these customers based?
- Will they want to repeat purchase?

(b)

- Find out if business is feasible
- Discover customer needs
- Find out if right target market
- Find out if she can sell enough to cover costs
- See if she can meet demand
- Set a price

Mark scheme

1 mark for identifying a suitable question.
Do not give a mark just for repeating the question – it has to add something else.
Up to 3 marks for explaining why this question is suitable. For example, asking what type of product customers want to buy is important for Ling to ask to find out if there is a market for her product. (1 mark) It could indicate whether there would be a sufficient demand for her product that is being produced or if another alternative will meet customer needs better. (1 mark) If there is not enough demand the business idea may not be successful. (1 mark)

2. (a) Suggest one question that Ling Tan should be asking at this stage about the workers in her future business. (1)

    (b) Explain why she should ask this question. (3)

Indicative content

(a)

- What if the workers do not have the skills required for the job?
- How many workers might be needed?
- What sort of training will they need?
- How will I recruit additional workers?

(b)

- Specialised product
- Expensive
- Could make/ruin big occasion
- Attitude
- Run business if she is ill
- Training

Mark scheme

1 mark for identifying a suitable question.
Do not give a mark just for repeating the question – it has to add something else.
Up to 3 marks for explaining why this question is suitable. For example, asking whether workers have the skills needed is important because a specialised product is being made. This is likely to need workers with particular skills. (1 mark) If workers do not have these skills then they may need training or other workers may need to be hired. (1 mark) The skills of the workers could determine the success of the business, as a quality product that is different from those of competitors must be made. (1 mark)

3. (a) Suggest **one** question that Ling Tan should be asking at this stage about the finances of her future business. (1)

(b) Explain why she should ask this question. (3)

Indicative content

(a)

- What if I do not have enough start-up capital?
- How should I manage my finances?
- What sort of finance do I need?
- How much will raising this finance cost?
- What is the most appropriate source of finance for this business?

(b)

- Survival
- Cover costs
- Feasible business
- Cash flow problems
- Profit
- Business plan
- Future planning
- Decision whether to go ahead

Mark scheme

1 mark for identifying a suitable question.

Do not give a mark just for repeating the question – it has to add something else.

Up to 3 marks for explaining why this question is suitable. For example, asking whether she has enough funds will tell her whether she can start up the business as she hopes to. (1 mark) It could point to the need to raise further funds from others. (1 mark) Without enough funds the business may not be able to start or may have cash flow problems and if this can not be cannot solved, it may not be successful. (1 mark)

4. Which do you think are the **two** most important questions that Ling Tan should be asking herself? Justify your answer. (6)

Mark scheme

Level	Mark	Descriptor
	No mark	Non-rewardable material
Level 1	1–2	A choice will be made with justification. For example, 'The market and finance, as they are important for the success of the business'.
Level 2	3–4	A choice will be made with some developed justification. For example, 'Asking if there is a market for the product will indicate potential sales and profits. Asking whether there are sufficient start-up funds will indicate whether the business has a problem and needs to find extra funding'.
Level 3	5–6	A choice will be made with a clearly developed justification. For example 'Asking if there is a market for a product is vital for any new business. Without a market that will buy a product the product is highly unlikely to be successful. The product must meet the needs of the customers in this market or be changed to meet them. Finance is also vital. Many new businesses are profitable but fail because of cash flow. One of the main reasons for this is lack of sufficient start-up funds'.

Chapter 9: **Questions to be asked**

Ivor Khestikov has completed his engineering degree and has decided to set up his own business.

1   State one reason why he might not want to consider setting up as a butcher.

2   State one reason why he might want to open up his own amusement arcade.

3   State four resources he would need when operating an amusement arcade.

4   State one location that would be a good place to set up an amusement arcade.

5   State three ways in which he could attract customers to his business.

6   When might be the best time for him to open his business? Explain your answer.

7   List four 'what-if' questions that Ivor could ask.

8   State two reasons why Ivor could be successful.

9   State two reasons why Ivor's business might fail.

10   Explain two ways in which Ivor could minimise his risks.

Suggested answers

1 Because he has no knowledge of the business nor the skills.

2 Because he is an engineer so he'll understand the mechanical side and the product is a known seller.

3 Examples could be cash, staff, machines, heating, lighting and electricity for the machines.

4 He would need to set up close to where the target market (teenagers) was so somewhere like a seaside resort would be good or maybe within a shopping mall where there are a lot of people looking for entertainment.

5 Some of the attraction would be natural by way of location but he could use special offers on the purchase of tokens to use inside. Music and flashing displays will encourage people to look. By having regular situations where people win he will attract people to re-visit. By maintaining the machinery well or hiring the latest games he will attract customers.

6 Probably during the summer season when people travel and visit attractions more. This would aid his initial cash flow and help recover the money he's spent quite quickly.

7 'What-if' there are too few customers?, 'What-if' I'm sick?, 'What-if' the site closes down?, 'What-if' there's only enough custom during the busy season?, 'What-if' I got my calculations on costs wrong?, 'What-if' I cannot get staff?

8 It is the type of business that always does well, he can ensure the machinery is working well himself, the target market is always there and evolving and he is meeting a customer need for entertainment.

9 Competitors might offer something better, the business might be dependent on visitors to the area so weather plays a part, a new type of fashion craze may come along and costs may change so the business is no longer profitable.

10 He could minimise his risks by carrying out research. Primary research could involve talking with the target market about what they want. He could try to ensure that he has enough finance to cover times of the year when custom might fall off and his revenue will be low, which could lead to cash flow problems.

Chapter 10: Invention and innovation

1. Jeff Briggs, an entrepreneur, spends £10,000 taking a recipe for a new chocolate cake through manufacture of the product to first sales to customers. This process would an example of

   A   innovation

   B   a patent

   C   copyright

   D   branding

   Select **one** answer.

   Answer A

Comments
A Correct – he went from just an idea to getting it to the customers.
B Incorrect – a patent is a legal right of the owner to produce a product, idea or process.
C Incorrect – copyright is not a process.
D Incorrect – it is about a recipe of a new chocolate cake – we are not told if it has a brand name.

2. A small business has developed a new type of product. It can best legally protect its discovery by

   A   more new inventions

   B   innovation

   C   developing a brand

   D   taking out a patent

   Select **one** answer.

   Answer D

Comments
A Incorrect – more new inventions would not help protect this one.
B Incorrect – innovation is not about legal protection.
C Incorrect – branding is about marketing and is not a form of legal protection.
D Correct – this makes copying the product illegal.

3. Three musicians have got together to form a group. They compose some original songs. Their songs can legally be protected through

    A   patents

    B   copyright

    C   innovation

    D   invention

Select **one** answer.

Answer B

Comments
A Incorrect – patents are about products.
B Correct – copyright is about the legal protection of ideas and material; this would mean that other people cannot play the songs without the group's permission.
C Incorrect – they have not tried to sell the songs.
D Incorrect – they are not inventing something – they are generating new musical ideas.

Chapter 10: Invention and innovation

Matthew and Claire Wyon own and run Flyte Ltd, a company which designs, assembles, markets and sells dance shoes, clothing and accessories. Matthew Wyon is a lecturer at Wolverhampton University in the School of Sport, Performing Arts and Leisure. Thanks to him, the university is now a major contributor to dance science research in the UK.

His company has used this research, and advances in the sports shoe industry, to develop a new type of ballet shoe. The shoe lasts longer than traditional ballet shoes. It improves the balance of the dancer. It also provides much better shock absorption when a dancer is jumping. Matthew and Claire have designed the shoe with the aim of reducing the number of foot and ankle injuries that are so common amongst ballet dancers.

The company has received over £100,000 in funding from investors to bring the new ballet shoe to market.

Source: adapted from the *Express & Star*, 20.10.2008.

1. Using Flyte Ltd as an example, explain what is meant by (a) invention and (b) innovation. (6)

Indicative content

Invention (must be features only, benefits are part of innovation)

- New **type** of ballet shoe
- Longer lasting
- New shock absorbing system
- Improves balance

Innovation

- £100,000 funding
- How they can take the idea but make it a commercial success
- Moving from an idea to making the shoe commercially viable – i.e. a shoe that is affordable and has a market
- Outside investors who believe in it/ willing to risk capital to help make it a success
- Known market
- Clear benefits to market need to be stressed – balance, fewer foot injuries

Mark scheme

1 mark each for a clear definition of invention and innovation. Up to 2 marks for explanation of how each applies to Flyte Ltd. For example, Invention is the discovery of new processes and potential new products. (1 mark) The new product or process typically comes after a period of research, which was the case with Flyte Ltd, which together with advances in technology, help to develop a new ballet shoe. (1 mark) The new shoe would have features that were not present in traditional shoes, such as improved durability, better balance and a new shock absorption system. (1 mark)

2. Define the term patent and explain how it can help Flyte Ltd protect its new ballet shoe. Explain your reasons. (3)

Indicative content

- Protect technology
- Prevents copying
- Monopoly for a period
- USP

Mark scheme

1 mark for definition of a patent. Up to 2 marks for explanation of how it can help Flyte Ltd protect its ballet shoe. For example, A patent gives right of ownership of an invention or process when it is registered with the government. (1 mark) If a patent is take out it prevents other businesses from copying the product, usually for a period of time. (1 mark) This allows business to sell its product with little competition and recover its often high costs of development. (1 mark)

3. Innovation is very expensive. Do you think that Flyte Ltd should continue to innovate? Justify your answer. (6)

Indicative content

Yes

- New products always needed
- Enough funding
- Benefits clearly identified
- Outside investors
- Spreads risk
- Reputation built

No

- Might not catch on
- Existing competition may be too strong
- Nothing known about price
- How big is the market?
- Can costs be recovered?
- Part-time business, could they meet demand?
- Production?

Mark scheme

Level	Mark	Descriptor
	No mark	Non-rewardable material
Level 1	1–2	A choice will be made with poorly developed justification and supported by limited examples. For example, 'Yes because there is a market for the new shoe.'
Level 2	3–4	A choice will be made with some developed justification and supported by some good examples. For example, 'Flyte Ltd may think that the cost and risk of innovation is high. But it should still continue to innovate. There is a market for this product and a need for a safer shoe. This could give Flyte enough of a competitive advantage if they manage to develop the product successfully.'
Level 3	5–6	A choice will be made with a clearly developed justification which is balanced and is supported by excellent examples. For example, 'Innovation is always risky and expensive. There is a high cost of bringing new products to market. The idea for the shoes might not work or catch on and time and money may be wasted. However, Flyte will need to spend money on making the product commercially viable if it wants to be successful. The fact that this is a product targeting a particular market and has a number of key features and support is likely to make it more successful. Flyte can develop a competitive advantage over its rivals and so should continue to innovate.'

Chapter 10: Invention and innovation

1   What is meant by the term 'invention'?

2   What is meant by the term 'innovation'?

3   What is the difference between a patent and a copyright?

4   An insurance company uses a song in its television advertisement without permission from the writers of the song. Is this a breach of copyright, patent or trademark?

5   Are the McDonald's two yellow arches an example of copyright, patent or trademark?

6   When Apple launched the iPod what might it have taken out to protect the technology behind it - copyright, patent or trademark?

7   State one reason why some inventions might not become innovations.

8   State two reasons how inventions might occur.

9   Explain why the invention of a battery that lasted forever is unlikely to be innovated.

10 State three reasons why an inventor of a new computer operating system might choose to let someone else carry out the innovation.

Suggested answers

1   Invention is finding out or creating something which has not existed before.

2   Innovation is adapting the invention so that it can be of use to consumers and making it commercially viable, thereby making it marketable.

3   A patent is the right of ownership of an invention or process which prevents other businesses from copying the invention or process. Copyright is the legal ownership of material in books or films for examples that prevents others from copying it.

4   Copyright.

5   Trademark.

6   Patent.

7   Reasons could include inability to produce the item at a price that consumers can afford, fashion, danger and demand might not exist.

8   Reasons could include by accident, demand, need for them and as a result of deliberate creativity.

9   This is because it is likely to reduce the amount of repeat purchases to zero. After a time the innovator may no longer get any income from sales. Most products rely on having to be replaced leading to repeat custom. An everlasting battery would also need to be expensive to cover the costs of production and the fact that there would be no repeat purchase means that it would probably not be viable.

10 This might be because someone else would have better skills at marketing the product and would probably have an established name that consumers would trust and buy from. The inventor might prefer to concentrate on the invention as the main aspect of their work. The inventor may not have the financial ability to get the product to the market. The inventor might not be totally confident that it will sell and so might not want to run the risk of innovation.

Chapter 11: **Taking a calculated risk**

1. Dylan runs a restaurant. Which **one** of the following would be an example of a calculated risk for his business?

    Select **one** answer.

    A   There is a 50:50 chance that he would lose over 10 per cent of his customers if he put up his prices by a fifth

    B   A customer might not like a new recipe

    C   The price of fish might go up by a quarter over the next 12 months

    D   The insurance bill for his business has increased by 10 per cent

    Answer A

Comments
A Correct – he has put a value on the risk and can make a decision based on that.
B Incorrect – a customer can buy something else.
C Incorrect – the price will go up anyway and will affect all restaurants.
D Incorrect – this does not relate to the probability of an event occurring – Dylan knows it will occur.

2. Javier runs a small business that makes wooden toys for sale by mail order and over the Internet, as well as to toy shops and gift companies. Which **one** of the following would be an example of an upside for his business?

    Select **one** answer.

    A   A rise in the wages he pays to his staff

    B   An increase in the cost of postage

    C   A rise in taxes on toys

    D   A fall in the price of wood

    Answer D

Comments
A Incorrect – this would be a downside – it would increase his costs of production.
B Incorrect – a rise in postage costs has to be passed on to consumers who may choose not to buy from him as a result.
C Incorrect – this would be a downside – it would mean he has to pay out more in tax.
D Correct – this would make the cost of making the toys cheaper.

3. Alicia runs a hairdressing business. Which **one** of the following would be an example of a downside for her business?

Select **one** answer.

A   A fall in the prices she has to pay her suppliers for hair care products

B   A rise in the wages she pays her staff

C   A rise in the number of her customers

D   A fall in the rent she pays on her business premises

Answer B

Comments
A Incorrect – this is an upside as her costs have fallen.
B Correct – her costs have risen.
C Incorrect – this is an upside and profits will rise.
D Incorrect – her fixed costs have fallen so her profits will rise.

Chapter 11: Taking a calculated risk

Nicky Mullinder works for a small engineering company. In her spare time, she has come up with an idea for a new type of can opener. She is investigating whether or not to leave her job and set up a business that would make and sell the new can opener.

Nicky has gone on a course provided by the local Business Link on setting up a business. Business Link is an organisation that provides help and advice for small businesses. Before she went on the course, she was very optimistic about this new business. She dreamt of selling millions of can openers a year. There would be a large factory making the can openers with a number of people working for her. Money from sales would flow into the business and she would earn a large profit. Then she would have enough money to buy a luxury car and a large house.

However, the course has made her much more pessimistic. Making a few can openers by hand in her home would be very different from making thousands every day in a factory. She had done no market research on whether customers liked her invention. She had no idea where the money would come from to start up her business. Giving up her job with a steady salary would be a huge risk since there was no guarantee that she would earn a single penny in her new business. In fact, there was a good chance that the business would make a loss and her new can opener would never become a popular product.

1. Explain **two** possible upsides to Nicky's possible new business. (6)

Indicative content

- High sales
- Profit
- Financial objectives
- Working for herself
- Employing lots of people
- Buying luxuries

Mark scheme

Up to 2 marks for identifying two possible upsides - the advantages of a course of action, including what can go right. Up to 2 marks for an explanation of how each applies to Nicky's new business. For example, 'One upside could be high sales. (1 mark) Nicky anticipated selling of selling millions of can openers a year. (1 mark) High sales would make the business very successful and profitable.' (1 mark)

2.   Explain **two** possible downsides to Nicky's possible new business.   (6)

Indicative content

- No market research
- No business plan
- No suppliers
- Might not be able to meet demand
- No idea about success/failure rates
- No experience
- Would need to patent (cost)

Mark scheme

Up to 2 marks for explaining two possible downsides - the disadvantages of a course of action, including what can go wrong. Up to 2 marks for an explanation about how each applies to Nicky's new business. For example, One downside could be a lack of market research. (1 mark) Nicky did no market research on whether customers liked her invention. She may find that, as a result there is no market for her product. (1 mark) If people do not like the product it may never become popular and the business might not be successful. (1 mark)

3.   (a) Define the term 'calculated risk'.   (1)

(b) Explain why Nicky should apply the principle of calculated risk to her business proposition.(3)

Mark scheme

(a) I mark for defining the principle of calculated risk.

(b)

Indicative content

- Put a value on whether a profit could be made
- Decide if worth going ahead
- See if earn more than at present
- Find out success/failure of similar ventures
- Minimise chances of failure
- Has no other quantitative evidence

Mark scheme

Up to 2 marks for explaining why Nicky should use this principle. For example, the principle of calculated risk involves estimating the probability of a negative event occurring. Using this might help Nicky to decide on the chances of success or failure of the business. (1 mark) She will then be in a better position to evaluate whether it will be worth going ahead with her plans; she would be able to get some idea of the size of the risk and make a decision about whether she wants to take that risk. (1 mark)

4. In your opinion, what are the **two** most important things that Nicky now needs to do if she is serious about setting up a business making can openers? Justify your answer. (6)

Indicative content

- Market research for demand
- Level of production
- Location
- Cash flow forecast
- Backing/ partners
- Part time?
- Research similar ventures
- Ownership?
- Evaluate risk
- List downsides
- List upsides
- Suppliers

Mark scheme

Level	Mark	Descriptor
	No mark	Non-rewardable material
Level 1	1–2	Up to two options will be given but there will be no development of either or one option is given with only a limited development, for example: 'She needs to find out of there is a market as some people may not want her can opener.'
Level 2	3–4	Two options will be given with some development of each. Or one option will be given with some reasoned development and evaluative comment to support the answer. For example, 'Nicky needs to identify whether there is a market or not. Market research will help her to do this. She also needs to consider where her funds would come from and whether she will have any cash flow problems. Both of these are vital for a successful business.'
Level 3	5–6	Two options will be given with some well reasoned development of both supported by excellent examples. For example, 'Nicky needs to produce a carefully thought out business plan. The business plan should consider aspects of the business and its potential market. For instance, Nicky needs to decide if, in fact, there is a market for can openers by surveying potential customers and other forms of market research. She also needs to carefully plan out her cash flow, evaluate whether her funds are sufficient and if not, where she will get further funding. Only by producing these plans will she be able to decide whether the business will be successful and whether she should leave her job.'

Chapter 11: Taking a calculated risk

1   What is meant by the term 'probability'?

2   What is meant by the term 'calculated risk'?

3   What is meant by the term 'downsides' to a business?

4   What is meant by the term 'upsides' to a business?

5   State two downsides of setting up a business renting out luxury cars.

6   State two upsides of teachers setting up a 'revision school'.

7   'A business has a 10% chance of success.' What does this mean?

8   State one reason why existing entrepreneurs tend to be more successful in setting up new businesses than first-time entrepreneurs.

9   Explain why a business plan might help an entrepreneur who faces risks when setting up a new business.

10 Sherrie Damon is thinking of setting up a ladies' store selling leather coats and handbags. Her research shows that she has an 80% chance of success. Do you think that should she go ahead?

Suggested answers

1 Probability is the likelihood of an event happening. The higher the probability the more likely it is to happen.

2 Calculated risk is a numerical value to help decide whether an idea is likely to succeed. It balances out the risk involved against the reward and gives the entrepreneur the basis on which to make a decision.

3 Downsides are the disadvantages of a course of action, including things that can go wrong.

4 Upsides are the advantages of a course of action, including things that could, and should, go well.

5 The downside hinges on the fact that it is a luxury business. The cars are very expensive to buy so there is a large financial investment needed. In times of economic slowdown this is the sort of expense many people choose to do without. Further, when renting something out there is always a greater risk of damage as the person using the car will be less careful than if it was their own. Having the car in for repair means it is not earning money so profits will fall. Also, selling these cars at the end of their usefulness is not always easy.

6 A revision school is a business that teachers know well if they chose to set one up, so they will know what is wanted. The teachers can employ other teachers so they can make money without doing the teaching. In most cases there may be 'reserve experts' available so unforeseen circumstances will not be a problem. Because they are working for themselves they can work what hours suit them and their lifestyle best. Lastly, they can set their own prices and rules meaning they do not have to take customers who are not reasonable to deal with.

7 It means that it has only a 10% or 1 in 10 chance of success. This is a low chance of success.

8 This is usually because they have experience and because they have learned from past mistakes. They know when things are going well and not well and when to move a business on. They will set targets based on more realistic calculated risks.

9 A business plan is a document that outlines the future of a business. It will include the upsides (what can go right) and the downsides (what can go wrong). This will help the entrepreneur to decide if the business is too risky and the chance of success, for example if there are many downsides.

10 Yes, she should because she is more likely to succeed. There is a fairly high chance that she will succeed (80%) and a fairly low chance (20%) chance of failure.

Chapter 12: Important enterprise skills

Mike Noake is a plumber and he has just set up his own business offering plumbing services mainly to households.

1. Which **one** of the following is most likely to be an example of Mike Noake showing the enterprise skill of 'planning'???

   Select **one** answer.

   A   Answering the phone from a customer who has a leaking pipe

   B   Buying a pipe at a plumbers' merchant

   C   Calculating how much he needs to save to replace his van in twelve months' time

   D   Drawing up the bill for a customer who has had his central heating fixed

   Answer C

Comments
A Incorrect – this happens when a problem arises and is not planned.
B Incorrect – this relates to everyday purchases that Mike has to make rather than looking ahead.
C Correct – he is looking ahead at something he will have to do twelve months in the future - putting money aside so the cost is already partly funded.
D Incorrect – this takes place after the job has been completed rather than some time before.

2. Which **one** of the following is most likely to be an example of Mike Noake showing the enterprise skill of 'seeing opportunities'?

   Select **one** answer.

   A   Driving to the home of a customer to fix a leaking basin

   B   Contacting a local house builder about doing some work for him

   C   Changing his mobile phone contract

   D   Getting his van repaired after an accident

   Answer B

Comments
A Incorrect – he is doing a job that he has been asked to do rather than seeking opportunities.
B Correct – he realises somebody has to do the plumbing so he could do it – Mike is looking for work that might exist in the future.
C Incorrect – it does not relate to seeking out new work.
D Incorrect – this is something he needs to do to keep the business running.

Test yourself answers
Topic 1.2: Showing enterprise

BUSINESS

3. Which **one** of the following is most likely to be an example of Mike Noake showing the enterprise skills of 'drive and determination'?

Select **one** answer.

A   Phoning a local house builder five times to see if he has any work for him

B   Filling his van up with petrol every week

C   Arranging insurance for his business once a year

D   Paying his tax on time every month

Answer A

Comments
A Correct – he is not prepared to give up.
B Incorrect – he has to do this to be able to get to clients.
C Incorrect – he has to pay this by law.
D Incorrect – he does this as part of running the business to keep his records correct.

Chapter 12: Important enterprise skills

More and more businesses are closing down. Unemployment is climbing. Sales of new cars are half what they were last year. You would have thought that now is not the time to start a new business. However, Jamie Speke has bucked the trend and launched out on his own.

Jamie has worked for three small engineering firms in his career. In his last job, he was the manager of a small company that made most of its money from maintenance contracts. The company would sign a deal with a customer to give 24 hour 7 day a week service. If a customer's machine broke down, he would go out and repair the machine.

However, Jamie had become frustrated with the company that employed him. The owners did not want to take any risks and were not interested in expanding the business. So he made plans to set up his own business. An opportunity came when a rival business was forced to close. It had been very badly run and Jamie was able to buy its building and machines for a knock down price.

His first priority was to keep the firm's existing customers. Equally important, he went out and found new customers. Some of the more skilled workers were re-employed and new ways of working were introduced which cut costs. By raising sales and cutting costs, Jamie has been able to turn the business around in its first twelve months of operation. It has been hard work for Jamie, but having drive and determination has helped him establish a successful business.

1. Jamie Speke has a number of enterprise skills. Explain **three** of these enterprise skills. (9)

Indicative content

Planning

- own business
- new techniques
- knew there were not enough customers

Thinking ahead

- realised own frustration
- keep skilled workers
- he has management skills
- customers of 'old' business still exist
- new techniques / stay up to date

Seeing opportunities

- state of economy
- cheap price
- buyer's market
- established company
- client base
- had the knowledge
- business had to get better

Drive and determination

- his decision and money
- need to prove himself
- financial objectives
- could measure success (profit)

Mark scheme

Up to 3 marks for identifying appropriate enterprise skills (1 mark for each skill) Up to 2 marks for development of each skill and application to Jamie. For example, 'Jamie was able to think ahead. (1 mark) He realised that he had abilities that he was not using effectively in his current job and that there were problems in the current operations. (1 mark) He could see that by setting up his own business he could improve on the problems that faced his current business, such as a lack of expansion and a lack of willingness to take risks to ensure success'. (1 mark)

2. Analyse **two** reasons why buying a 'rival business' was a **good** way for Jamie to establish his own successful business. (8)

Indicative content

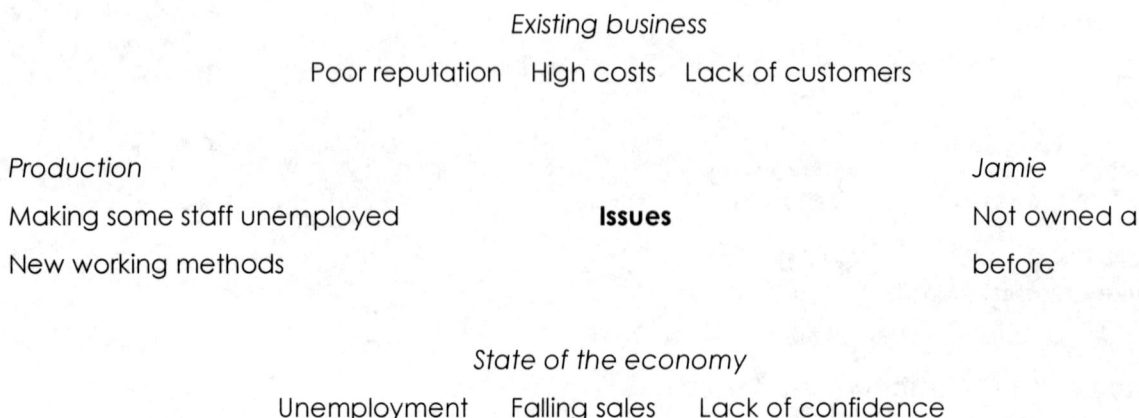

- Already a garage
- Client base/customers
- Had built a reputation/loyalty but losing it
- Location known to customers
- Price
- if he can make it work in the bad times then can only improve
- Existing workforce with skills
- Denies someone else the opportunity
- Knows the competition

Mark scheme

Up to 2 marks for identifying appropriate reasons. (1 mark for each) Up to 3 marks for development of each reason. For example, 'Buying an existing business means there is an existing workforce. (1 mark) They know the business and will have experience of the good and bad points of its operation. (1 mark) Hiring the best of these workers saves the cost of recruitment and training for new workers. (1 mark) These workers will be more familiar with the business and the customers and this in addition to their skills will help Jamie establish the business quickly. (1 mark)

3. Construct a mindmap to show the factors and issues faced by Jamie when setting up his new business. (6)

Indicative content

Existing business

Poor reputation   High costs   Lack of customers

Production		Jamie
Making some staff unemployed	**Issues**	Not owned a
New working methods		before

State of the economy

Unemployment   Falling sales   Lack of confidence

Mark scheme

1 mark for diagram. Up to 5 marks for appropriate issues.

Chapter 12: Important enterprise skills

1   Entrepreneurs are often said to be driven. What is meant by the term 'driven' in business?

2   What is a mindmap?

3   'There was a good opportunity for a new business.' What is meant by the phrase 'good opportunity'?

4   In a village people always had to go out to cafes and restaurants to eat. What might be one business opportunity?

5   State three examples of business opportunities in the area in which you live.

6   State one advantage to a business of effective planning.

7   'Peter ordered more cards for his gift shop just before Christmas.' Why is this an example of an entrepreneur planning ahead?

8   State three ideas that you might include on a mindmap of how you study.

9   State four ideas that might appear on a mindmap for a new toy product.

10 State two ways in which an entrepreneur who felt that they were weak at keeping their accounts could solve this problem.

Suggested answers

1 In business, this means being very motivated and determined to succeed.

2 A mind map is a diagram or graphical image using words to clarify ideas, tasks, or other items linked to a central key word or idea.

3 An opportunity is a chance or possibility. A good opportunity is a good chance for a business to be set up.

4 If all people had to go out to eat, then an opportunity might be to set up a take –away service.

5 This will vary depending on your street or road, or if you live in a remote area, but could include a window cleaning service, a cash wash service, paper, milk or food delivery, gardening service or tree felling.

6 An advantage of effective planning is that it helps to keep risks to a minimum and puts in place plans (contingencies) to cover problems that might occur which might otherwise stop the venture.

7 Planning ahead means taking into account what might happen in future. Peter ordered cards for his gift shop because people tend to buy cards at Christmas. He would have to buy in cards to make sure they were in the shop when people needed them.

8 This will vary from one person to another, but could include organised/disorganised, work with people/work alone, at night/in the day.

9 Ideas could include shape, colour, materials and function.

10 They might solve the weakness in accounting by employing an accountant. They might take classes in accounting to improve their own accounting. They might employ someone who had accounting skills.

Practice exam questions

Jason Stait was angry. He was in a restaurant and the service was slow. It wasn't that the waiters weren't working hard, they were. It was the fact that they seemed to waste so much time running back and forward to the kitchen, the till and the phone.

Jason began to think creatively about the problem and came up with the idea of 'i-Waiter'. This would be an electronic device by which waiters could send orders directly to the kitchen. It would have a 'time-received' feature, so the kitchen could prioritise orders. When an order was ready a message would flash on the device to inform the waiter to collect and serve. At the end of the meal the waiter could use the stored order information to produce a bill and accept chip-and-pin payment.

Jason approached his friend Richey Sugg, who was an electronics expert, to help develop the product because he lacked technical knowledge. Jason just knew it would work and hoped that he could leave his job and set up a successful enterprise. Jason had not run a business before, but thought that he had the determination and drive to be successful. Jason did some research and found there was no other product like it. A local restaurant tried it out and agreed Jason was on to a winner. He produced a business plan which showed that he would have to spend a lot of money to develop the product.

1. Which **two** of the following would Jason be **most likely** to do **before** deciding whether to launch the i-Waiter?

   A Design a flyer to advertise it
   B Get a patent to protect the idea
   C Assess the idea using lateral thinking
   D Sell shares on the stock exchange to raise money
   E Use his savings to buy a restaurant
   F Check out the existing competition

Answer B and C

Examiner's comment
A Incorrect – he has not yet made the decision about whether to go ahead.
B Correct – he needs to protect the design from other people who might try to get in ahead of him with it.
C Correct – he will then have thought about the idea from all angles before spending any money on it
D Incorrect – there is no business yet.
E Incorrect – he doesn't need to own a restaurant for this to be successful.
F Incorrect – currently there is no direct competition.

2. Identify and explain **two** questions that Jason t, as an entrepreneur, needs to ask about his new business idea. (6)

Indicative content

- Why?
- Why not?
- What if?
- Is there really a market?
- What personal qualities are required?
- What risks are there?

Mark scheme

Identification of two questions that Jason might ask (up to 2 marks). Two further marks for development of each question. For example, one question Jason might ask is 'Why am I doing this?' (1 mark) By asking this question he is helping herself to clarify what his aims might be (1 mark) and this helps him to plan more effectively.' (1 mark)

3. Do you think that the risks are too great for Jason to go ahead and set up his business? Justify your answer. (6)

Indicative content

Downsides/risks too great/against setting up

- Lacks technical knowledge
- High cost of setting up if business fails
- Has not set up a business before and lacks experience
- May not get a patent and competition could join the market
- Giving up her job
- Limited sample for research

Upsides/risks not too great/for setting up

- Richey can compensate for Jason's lack of knowledge
- No competition at present
- Could protect idea with a patent
- Could return to job if business fails
- Has drive and determination if facing setbacks
- Research indicates product works and people will buy it
- Product has a USP, which could be attractive to businesses like restaurants

Mark scheme

Level	Mark	Descriptor
	No mark	Non-rewardable material
Level 1	1–2	A limited attempt is made to justify a decision, for example, 'Jason should not set up because the risks are too high due to his lack of experience.'
Level 2	3–4	A decision is made with some justification, for example, 'Jason should not set up in business. The risks are quite high. He has only carried out a limited amount of research and the product may not be a successful innovation when brought to market. The initial costs are high and he may not be able to cover these when he returns to work.'
Level 3	5–6	A decision is given with some evaluative comment in support of the decision including the degree of risk being estimated. For example, 'Jason should not set up in business. There are clearly risks, such as the high costs at the start of developing the product. Jason lacks technical and business experience. Although he has drive and determination and can use Richey's skills, this may not compensate for his lack of experience. Success may depend on whether a patent can be obtained. Without it other businesses could copy the idea. The limited amount of research could be problem and the product may not be a successful innovation when brought to market.'

Case study

Claire Critchlow worked in salons and as a mobile beautician. Now she is setting up her own beauty salon in a former doctor's surgery. The salon will offer services and products such as manicures, pedicures, spray tans, sun beds and permanent make-up. Claire's objective to start with is to survive the first year. Then she hopes the business will make a profit and she can open more salons. Facing a challenge and doing something new have always given Claire personal satisfaction. Setting up on her own, as a mobile beautician, gave her a sense of achievement. Now she wants to build something bigger.

Taking on staff will allow Claire to show leadership qualities. She will also need determination and initiative. The project will test her ability to plan, make decisions and take sensible risks. Claire has the backing of a business adviser, Rachael, from a government agency, Business Link. She helped Claire get on courses to develop the skills she would need to set up in business on her own. Rachael also helped Claire to write a business plan. This is a document that covers all aspects of the business, including finance, marketing and people. In the finance part, Claire had to estimate revenues and costs for the first two years of trading. From this, she was able to forecast the profit for the next two years. She also produced a cash flow forecast. This showed how revenues and costs would affect the amount of cash still in the business. The cash flow forecast was vital for survival of the salon. If it ran out of cash, it would be forced to close.

Setting up the business required cash. It was needed for converting the surgery, advertising and buying in equipment. Although Claire rented the premises, the landlord wanted a deposit up front. Claire had some savings of her own that she put into the business. Her father gave her some money. She borrowed the rest from the bank.

Success will require hard work and determination from Claire, as well as luck. She has taken advice and prepared a business plan. These will improve her chances of survival in the short term and her success in the long term.

Suggested discussion points/answers

1. Why did Claire want to set up a business?

Possible reasons could include:

- Survive (financial)
- Make a profit (financial)
- Challenge (non-financial)
- Personal satisfaction (non-financial)

2. What qualities did she have that might have made her a successful entrepreneur?

Possible qualities could include:

- Leadership in running the staff
- Planning and determination to put it into effect. You can plan well, but doing it is another matter.
- Decision making skills
- Risk taking abilities
- Balancing/ trading off risks against decisions

3. Why was estimating future revenues, costs, profits and cash flows important for Claire?

Possible reasons could include:

- Spotting months where difficulties can emerge
- Make contingency plans/ take remedial action
- Check whether her estimates (her planning skills) matched actual outcomes.
- Decide whether the business will make sufficient profits to be worthwhile.

4. How did Claire raise the money to start to her business?

Possible methods could include:

- Savings (could be used for short-term costs)
- Family (capital) (could be used for short term costs)
- Bank loan (long term)

Chapter 13: **Objectives when starting up**

1. Which of the following are the most likely reasons why individuals would want to start a business?

    Select **three** answers.

    A   To increase their earnings

    B   They dislike taking risks

    C   Because they enjoy a challenge

    D   To give them greater control over their future

    E   They prefer to work for someone else

    F   They are afraid of failure

    G   Because they have followed a course in business studies

    Answer A, C and D

Comments
A Correct – they keep all the money that they earn.
B Incorrect – any new business involves a risk.
C Correct – they enjoy the thrill of risk and the rewards that go with it.
D Correct – they may do work for someone else and lack control.
E Incorrect – starting your own business has a high risk factor.
F Incorrect – an entrepreneur starting a business must accept risk and possible failure.
G Incorrect – simply following a course in business is not a requirement to start a business.

2. Which of the following would be a non-financial objective for individuals to start a business?

    Select **one** answer.

    A   To increase income

    B   To get greater work satisfaction

    C   To accumulate wealth

    D   To maximise profit

    Answer B

Comments
A Incorrect – this is a financial objective.
B Correct – they are doing what they want, when they want. This is a non-financial objective.
C Incorrect – this is a financial objective
D Incorrect – this is a financial objective

Read the passage below carefully and then answer question 3 which relates to the passage.

Kim Lawton has just set up a restaurant in London. She wants the business to be profitable within six months. After that, she hopes profits will increase sufficiently for her to open a second restaurant within two years. Her personal objective is to own a small chain of restaurants within five years which would make her a wealthy person earning a large amount of money.

3. Which of the following personal objectives does Kim have in opening her restaurant, according to the passage?

    Select **two** answers.

    A   To give customer service

    B   To increase her income

    C   To let someone else make the decisions

    D   To become wealthy

    E   To help others

Answer B and D

Comments
A Incorrect – her main objectives are financial rather than to give customer service which is non-financial. This is not mentioned in the passage.
B Correct – she wants to keep all the income/ profit for herself.
C Incorrect – this is not mentioned in the passage. Passing decision making to another person is likely to fit in with her objective to make profitable business for herself.
D Correct – this is an objective she has stated as part of starting off on her own.
E Incorrect – her main objectives are financial rather than to help others which is non-financial. This is not mentioned in the passage.

Chapter 13: Objectives when starting up

When Emma Ratner graduated from university after getting a pharmacy degree, she went to work for a large chain of chemists. Her ambition, though, was always to have her own pharmacy. With financial help from her family and a bank loan, she was able to buy a pharmacy after five years. She was determined to repay the loan as quickly as possible and become financially independent. Within two years, she had increased the profits of the pharmacy 50 per cent by increasing the amount of stock available for sale in the shop. Soon, she was looking to buy a second pharmacy so she could increase her profits further

Peter Shannon graduated too with a pharmacy degree. Like Emma, he began his working career as a pharmacist at a large high street chain. But it took him ten years to buy his own pharmacy. He enjoyed the contact his own pharmacy gave him with customers. The shop gave him a good profit. But he saw giving a service to the local community as more important than earning extra profit.

1. Explain **one** financial objective that Emma Ratner might have had in buying her pharmacy. *(3)*

Indicative content

Financial objectives may have been:

- to make a profit – so that the business can survive – gives the business funds to grow in future;
- to repay the loan – so that Emma is no longer in debt – can be financially independent.

Mark scheme

An appropriate objective is given why Emma Ratner might have bought her own pharmacy (1 mark) and this is explained. For example, 'Emma wanted to repay the loan as quickly as possible (1 mark). Repaying the loan would remove the debt from the business (1 mark). Emma would now be financially independent and more able to make her own decisions.' (1 mark)

2. Explain **one** non-financial objective that Peter Shannon might have had when buying his pharmacy. *(3)*

Indicative content

Non-financial objectives may have been:

- to help people;
- personal satisfaction.

Mark scheme

An appropriate non-financial objective is given why Peter Shannon might have bought his own pharmacy and this is explained. For example, 'Peter wanted to provide a service to the community. (1 mark) He wanted to help when they were feeling ill (1 mark). He felt that his training and experience would allow his pharmacy to provide very good advice to customers and this was more important than making a profit.' (1 mark)

Over to you answers
Topic 1.3: Putting a business idea into practice
BUSINESS

3. Compare the personal objectives of Emma Ratner with Peter Shannon in setting up and running their own businesses. *(6)*

Indicative content

- Emma more profit orientated than Peter – wanted to become financially independent and expand the business.
- Peter more concerned about customers – enjoyed contact with customers.
- Emma more ambitious - bought business after five years compared to Peter's ten.

Mark scheme

Level	Mark	Descriptor
	No mark	Non-rewardable material
Level 1	1–2	A similarity or difference is stated but supported by limited explanation. For example, 'Peter is not interested in money but Emma is'.
Level 2	3–4	A similarity or difference is stated, supported by some good explanation. For example, 'Emma seems mostly motivated by the profits that she can make from her business whilst Peter is more interested in the service he can provide. Emma has financial motives but Peter has non-financial motives.'
Level 3	5–6	Similarities and differences are clearly explained, supported by examples. For example, 'Emma is financially motivated by running her business. She has expanded the business quickly and this will help her to make further profit in the future. Peter wants to make a profit – he has to survive, but financial rewards are not the primary motivator. He enjoys the role he plays in the community and the service that he provides. This is a non-financial motive for running a business.

4. Do you think that Peter Shannon should buy a second pharmacy like Emma Ratner? Justify your answer. *(6)*

Indicative content

No

- He would lose personal contact.

Yes

- He could develop a better service in any community.
- He could make more profit.
- He could reinvest.

Mark scheme

Level	Mark	Descriptor
	No mark	Non-rewardable material
Level 1	1–2	A choice will be made with poorly developed justification and supported by limited examples. For example, 'No – he doesn't want to.'
Level 2	3–4	A choice will be made with some developed justification and supported by some good examples. For example, 'Peter should not buy a second pharmacy because his primary concern is the service he provides to his community. A second pharmacy might take him away from his customers.'
Level 3	5–6	A choice will be made with a clearly developed justification and supported by excellent examples. For example, 'Peter could open a second pharmacy. Given his main motive is to provide a service this would mean he could provide a good quality service to even more people. This might increase his job satisfaction even further.'

Chapter 13: **Objectives when starting up**

1   What is meant by the term 'financial objectives'?

2   What is meant by the term 'non-financial objectives'?

3   State two non-financial objectives.

4   State two financial objectives.

5   'Ingrid wants to earn £20,000 this year from the business.' Why is this a financial objective?

6   State one non-financial objective of a charity.

7   A new clothes shop has just opened. It only has a small number of customers and knows that it faces competition from larger shops in the area. What is most likely to be its main financial objective in the first year?

8   Intzar and Luke decide to leave their jobs as web designers to set up on their own. The main reason was that they were always being told what to do and felt that if they were able to make their own decisions their designs could be much better. What is most likely to be their main non-financial objective?

9   State two possible non-financial objectives of a funeral service.

10 Reyshe Croft worked for an insurance company but she was told there was no chance of promotion. Explain one financial reason and one non-financial reason why Reyshe might want to set up on her own.

Suggested answers

1   Financial objectives are targets for success set by a business when starting up that can be measured using numerical monetary units.

2   Non-financial objectives are qualitative targets that are not measured in money terms.

3   Examples of non-financial objectives include personal satisfaction, being your own boss, meeting and overcoming a challenge, beating the odds, proving people wrong, being independent and controlling what you do and when.

4   Examples of financial objectives include survival, making income and profit, wealth creation and financial security.

5   This is a financial objective as it is a target in money terms.

6   A charity might have the non-financial objective of helping others. People involved in charities often give of their time and resources to help others.

7   Its main objective is most likely to be survival as it faces a great deal of competition and only has a small number of customers.

8   Enjoying independence to make their own decisions and control of their own business could be their most likely objective.

9   Two objectives of a funeral service could be to have the satisfaction of providing an excellent service, to cater for the needs of families at difficult times and to remain as an independent business so that the owners could make their own decisions.

10 Reyshe would have a combination of objectives. Her non-financial objectives could be to prove to her present company that she could succeed so that would be a challenge to her. She would have control of her future instead of relying on someone else. At the same time promotion usually leads to more income and, as this has been denied to Reyshe, she may set herself financial objectives such as a higher income. Success in one type of objective will lead to success in the other.

Chapter 14: **The qualities shown by entrepreneurs**

1. In this question, match a quality of an entrepreneur, shown on the left, with an example of that quality, shown on the right. Each quality has only one example. Show each of your five answers by writing out a quality with the example of the quality.

Quality shown by entrepreneurs				Example of quality
Persuasion	1		a	Preparing a production schedule for the next four weeks
Initiative	2		b	Talking a supplier round to giving an extra 2 per cent discount on an order
Luck	3		c	Ordering in 20 per cent more stock in the hope that sales will increase shortly
Risk taking	4		d	Employing a worker who turns out to be much better and more skilled than expected
Planning	5		e	Following the loss of an important customer, deciding to prioritise getting more orders

Answer

1-b Persuasion – talking a supplier round to giving an extra 2 per cent discount on an order,
2-e Initiative – following the loss of an important customer, deciding to prioritise getting more orders.
3-d Luck – employing a worker who turns out to be much better and more skilled than expected.
4-c Risk taking – ordering in 20 per cent more stock in the hope that sales will increase shortly.
5-a Planning – preparing a production schedule for the next four weeks.

2. In this question, match a quality of an entrepreneur, shown on the left, with an example of that quality, shown on the right. Each quality has only one example. Show each of your five answers by writing out a quality with the example of the quality.

Quality shown by entrepreneurs				Example of quality
Determination	1		a	Reorganising the layout of the factory
Leadership	2		b	Talking a worker round to doing some overtime
Making decisions	3		c	Having been rejected for a loan by four banks, applying to another bank for the loan
Persuasion	4		d	An ice cream manufacturer has its best sales ever because of the hottest summer on record
Luck	5		e	Having a vision for where the business should be in two years' time

Answer

1-c Determination – having been rejected for a loan by four banks, applying to another bank for the loan.
2-e Leadership – having a vision for where the business should be in two years' time.
3-a Making decisions – reorganising the layout of the factory.
4-b Persuasion – talking a worker round to doing some overtime.
5-d Luck – an ice cream manufacturer has its best sales ever because of the hottest summer on record.

Chapter 14: **The qualities shown by entrepreneurs**

Michelle Welsman read a newspaper article about a business selling gift wrapping services. She immediately fell in love with the idea and began her research. She found there was no gift wrapping business in her own area and so there would be no competition. But then she began to worry about the money she could lose if her business was not a success. Going out with her new boyfriend also put a limit on the amount of time she could spend on the project. Her family said she should stick with her present job because it brought in a regular salary. Setting up in business was too risky. So she decided to start up the business using what spare time she had. To begin with, she targeted friends and family for orders. But not many orders came in and after six months she abandoned the idea of setting up a business.

Mai Ling Tsui lived in a different part of the country to Michelle. She too read the same newspaper article about a business offering gift wrapping services. Like Michelle, she saw this as a business opportunity. She took some time to research and prepare a business plan which saw her as working part-time in the business at the start, moving to full-time within two years once the business had become established. The plan enabled her to keep control over her costs more easily. Initial costs were kept to a minimum because the business was operated from home. Her only major cost was setting up a website and using the local paper for advertising. After two years, the business was profitable. But Mai Ling decided the profits were not good enough. So she moved on, setting up another business selling bridal gowns.

1. Explain how both Michelle and Mai Ling showed initiative after they had read about the newspaper article. *(3)*

Indicative content

- Initiative means making the first move.
- Means being a self-starter and pro-active.
- Read article - researched the market - set up businesses - Michelle in spare time, Mai Ling part-time.

Mark scheme
How Michelle and Mai Ling showed initiative will be identified (1 mark). Up to two further marks for explanation. For example, 'Michelle and Mai Ling both took initiative by making the first move. (1 mark). They did not wait to be told what to do. After reading the article they researched the market to find if there is an opportunity for a business (1 mark). They used this information to set themselves up in business – they actually made the move to do something about their idea.' (1 mark).

2. Explain how Mai Ling showed enterprise qualities in setting up her business. *(3)*

Indicative content

- Planning.
- Prepared to take risks.
- Make decisions.

Mark scheme
One enterprise quality showed by Mai Ling will be identified (1 mark) and explained (2 further marks). For example, 'Mai Ling showed good planning skills in setting up her business. (1 mark) She realised that a properly prepared and researched business plan would increase the chance that the business would be a success. (1 mark) She planned to keep costs to a minimum by working from home. This meant she was able to make more profit.' (1 mark).

3. Compare Michelle's entrepreneurial qualities with those of Mai Ling's: consider their attitude to risk, their decision making and planning skills and their self-confidence. *(8)*

Indicative content

- Both did some planning – Michelle = qualitative, Mai Ling = quantitative.
- Both went part-time to limit risk.
- Mai Ling more positive about outcomes.
- Michelle looked inward for safe customers (family).
- Mai Ling looked outward for new customers.
- Mai Ling had belief in herself and the product.
- Mai Ling spent more time planning and researching the business.
- Michelle did not really believe.
- Michelle not prepared to make social sacrifices than Mai Ling was.

Mark scheme

Level	Mark	Descriptor
	No mark	Non-rewardable material
Level 1	1–3	A similarity or difference is stated but supported by limited explanation. For example, 'Both Michelle and Mai Ling set up part-time at first' (would be worth just 1 mark.
Level 2	4–6	A similarity or difference is stated, supported by some good explanation. For example, 'Mai Ling and Michelle both decided to start the business on a part-time basis. This meant they could see how the business would develop whilst keeping their regular income. This would have helped them reduce the risk because if the business did not work they would still have some income to fall back on.'
Level 3	7–8	Similarities and differences are clearly explained, supported by examples. For example, 'Michelle tended to look at a wider market by looking outside her immediate family and friends which is what Michelle did. This gave her business a greater chance of success. She is also likely to have researched this market for her business plan and knew more about what her market would be. Michelle did not do this which may partly explain why her business did not succeed.'

4. Do you think that Mai Ling Tsui will make a success of her bridal business? Justify your answer. *(6)*

Indicative content

Yes

- Plans well.
- Takes calculated risks.
- Gives scheme time to work.
- Looks at whole market.
- Dedicated.
- Benchmarks 'success'.

No

- Track record is one of failure.
- May get nervous about risk this time.
- Luxury market/ credit crunch.
- May need to go full-time.
- High sunk costs in stock may hinder cash flow.

Mark scheme

Level	Mark	Descriptor
	No mark	Non-rewardable material
Level 1	1–2	A choice will be made with poorly developed justification and supported by limited examples. For example, 'Mai Ling's new business will be a success because she produces a business plan.'
Level 2	3–4	A choice will be made with some developed justification and supported by good examples. For example, 'Mai Ling plans her business carefully and this helps to reduce the risk of failure. Having gained experience from her first attempt she is more likely to be able to learn lessons and avoid making the same mistakes. She is determined enough to make this a more successful business.'
Level 3	5–6	A choice will be made with a clearly developed justification, supported by excellent examples. For example, 'Mai Ling has not really succeeded with the first business despite her careful planning and other enterprise qualities. It was not that she was making no profit but that they were not good enough. It may be that this business has a bigger market and this will allow her to make the larger profits that she wants. Her planning and the experience of the first business will help to reduce the risk of failure this time round so it might work.'

Chapter 14: **The qualities shown by entrepreneurs**

1   What is meant by the term 'initiative'?

2   What is meant by the term 'commitment'?

3   What is meant by the term 'risk-taker'?

4   What is meant by the term 'business plan'?

5   What is meant by the term 'self-confidence'?

6   Why does a business need a leader with 'a vision'?

7   'Entrepreneurs need to be good managers of time.' Explain what is meant by the term 'good time management'.

8   State two examples of good time management.

9   The owner of a shop has decided to stay open later to compete with supermarkets. His two staff are not happy. What type of entrepreneurial skills might he need to show?

10   Dwain 'Ice Party' Pomeroy thought there might be a market for an ice-based theme park combining winter skills with fun activities, but he is not certain. He asked his friend to do some research into it for him rather than doing it himself. Dwain is not sure he has all it takes to 'give it a go'. Explain why Dwain is unlikely to succeed.

Suggested answers

1   Initiative means taking control of the situation, making the first move. It is trying to shape the final outcome in the way you want.

2   Commitment means being fully focused on the plan, giving it 100% in terms of effort in every element not just in parts that suit or seems easy.

3   A risk-taker is someone who looks at the chances in a positive way and looks for reasons to do things rather than avoid them. Even if the probability of success is less than 50% the risk-taker may still be prepared to try and beat the odds.

4   A business plan is a document which entrepreneurs use to plan the future of their business and indicate to stakeholders how they will meet the objectives they have set. It can also be used to secure financial backing and will contain clear numerical estimates of sales and costs.

5   A person with self-confidence has total belief in what they are doing, that it is the right thing to do and the total belief that they are the right person to do it.

6   A business needs a leader with vision because someone who has clarity of thought, a clear idea of where they want to go and a belief in what they are doing helps to guide the business and carry everyone forward if things are not going.

7   Good time management is about organising your time to be productive and effective.

8   Examples of good time management include, knowing when you work best (morning, afternoon, evening or night), putting a limit on the amount of time allocated to a task to ensure it is done within that time frame, allocating time for breaks so that productivity is maintained and being very organised and able to prioritise effectively.

9   He might need to show skills of persuasion and good communication. Good entrepreneurs are able to persuade others to do what they want. He will have to persuade them that this is the best way to survive, faced with such competition.

10 Dwain is unlikely to succeed because he is not fully convinced about the product or about himself. If he was, he would do his own research so he knew what he was talking about. He would also be sure he has what it takes to 'give it a go'. He would be fully committed to the business and determined for it to succeed. He would be positive rather than lukewarm or negative. These examples show that Dwain believes the business will fail and he might be right.

Chapter 15: Estimating revenues, costs and profits

1. Which three of the following are examples of variable costs?

   Select **three** answers.

   A   Rent on a factory unit

   B   The cost of clothes bought by a high street fashion boutique

   C   Advertising in a local newspaper

   D   The salary of the managing director of a company

   E   Coca-Cola drinks in a fast food restaurant

   F   Diesel fuel used by a taxi driver

   G   The interest on a loan

   Answer B, E and F

Comments
A Incorrect – rent is a fixed cost which does not change regardless of how much is produced (output).
B Correct – the cost of clothes is a cost that increases or decreases with the number bought in by the shop.
C Incorrect – advertising in a local newspaper is a fixed cost which does not change as output changes. The cost will be incurred whether the sales change or not.
D Incorrect – the salary of the managing director of a company is a fixed cost which does not change as output changes.
E Correct – Coca-Cola drinks in a fast food restaurant are a variable cost which rises as more drinks are sold.
F Correct – diesel fuel used by a taxi driver is variable cost which rises as more taxi rides are made.
G Incorrect – the interest on a loan is a fixed cost which does not change as output changes.

2. A paintball business charges customers £10 for each paintball session. Last year customers paid for 5,000 sessions. This year, it increased its prices to £11 but the number of sessions sold fell to 4,000. What effect will this have had on revenues?

   Select **one** answer.

   Revenues will

   A   increase by 10 per cent

   B   fall by £10 000

   C   change from £50 000 to £44 000

   D   increase by £1,000

   Answer C

Comments
A Incorrect – revenues fall by 12% (£6,000 ÷ £50,000 × 100%).
B Incorrect – revenues fall by £6,000.
C Correct – revenues change from £50,000 (5,000 × £10) to £44,000 (4,000 × £11).
D Incorrect – revenues fall by £6,000.

3. A maker of electric guitars has fixed costs of £2,000 per month. Last month, it manufactured 50 guitars items. Its variable cost was £70 per guitar. This month, it has produced 60 guitars and the variable cost per guitar has stayed the same. What effect will this have on its total costs?

Select **one** answer.

Its total cost will increase

A by 20 per cent

B by £700

C from £3,500 to £4,200

D by £70

Answer B

Comments
A Incorrect – total costs increase by 13% (£700 ÷ £5,500 × 100%).
B Correct – total costs increase by £700. This is calculated by variable costs this month of 60 × £70 (£4,200) + fixed costs of £2,000 = £6,200 **minus** variable costs last month of 50 × £70 (£3,500) + fixed costs of £2,000 = £5,500.
C Incorrect – variable costs rise from £3,500 to £4,200.
D Incorrect – total costs rise by £700.

Chapter 15: **Estimating revenues, costs and profits**

Pets Havens is a business which is now two years old. Set up by Kevin and Emma, it provides a mobile pet-grooming service. They decided there was a gap in the market in their local area of Bournemouth and hope to expand the business to cover other services such as providing kennels for overnight accommodation for pets.

To start the business, they took out a loan for £20,000 repayable over five years. Most of this was used to pay for two vans. A small van transports equipment to allow grooming in the client's home. A large van acts as mobile premises and 'doggie makeovers' are given in the van itself. Around £5,000 was used to buy equipment for the business and set up a website. Kevin and Emma are paying back the loan at a rate of £400 per month.

They have a variety of other costs which stay the same however much work they complete. For example, they pay an accountant to sort out their finances. They have to pay insurance on their vans and for their business. They also advertise in *Yellow Pages*. These costs add up to £5,200 a year.

Each visit they make to a client costs money too. There are petrol costs as well as the cost of shampoos and other grooming materials. These costs work out at £5 per session.

The average price they charge clients is £20 per session. Kevin and Emma complete around ten sessions a day, which, by the time you take holidays into account, is 2,000 sessions a year.

1. Make a list of Kevin and Emma's (a) fixed costs and (b) variable costs in running their business that are mentioned in the passage. (4)

Indicative content

(a) Fixed costs include repayments on the loan, insurance, accountancy fees and advertising in *Yellow Pages*.

(b) Variable costs include petrol costs, shampoos and other grooming materials.

Mark scheme

1 mark for each example up to a maximum of 2 marks for each type of cost.

2. (a) How many pet grooming sessions do they sell each year? (b) What is the average price paid by customers for each pet grooming session? (c) What is Kevin and Emma's total sales revenue for the year? (3)

Indicative content

(a) 2,000

(b) £20

(c) Total sales are 2,000 × £20 = £40,000

Mark scheme

1 mark for each correct calculation.

3. Kevin and Emma have worked out that their total fixed costs are £10,000 per year. Explain how they calculated this. (3)

Indicative content

Their fixed costs are

- repayments on loan £400 per month × 12 = £4,800 a year
- other fixed costs are £5,200
- total fixed costs = £4,800 + £5,200 = £10,000

Mark scheme

I mark for each correct part of calculation

4. (a) What is their variable cost per pet grooming session? (b) What are their total variable costs per year? (2)

Indicative content

(a) £5 per session

(b) Number of sessions completed, 2,000, times the cost per session, £5. So total variable costs are £10,000

Mark scheme

I mark for each correct calculation

5. Calculate the value of their total costs. (3)

Indicative content

Total costs are:

- total fixed costs of £10,000 plus
- total variable costs of £10,000 equals
- £20,000 (£10,000 + £10,000)

Mark scheme

I mark for each correct part of calculation

6. How much profit do they make over a year giving 2,000 pet grooming sessions? (3)

Indicative content

- Total revenue = 2,000 x £20 = £40,000.
- Total costs = £10,000 + £10,000 = £20,000.
- Profit = £40,000 - £20,000 = £20,000

Mark scheme

I mark for each correct part of calculation

7. Would they have made a profit if they had only completed 400 sessions in a year? Explain your
answer. (6)

Indicative content and mark scheme

- Completing 400 sessions would have made a loss.
- Completing 400 sessions would have made a loss. (2 marks)
- Total revenue at 400 sessions would be 400 x £20 = £8,000. (1 mark)
- Total costs at 400 sessions would be fixed costs of £10,000 plus variable costs of 400 x £5 = £2,000. So total costs would be £10,000 + £2,000 = £12,000. (1 mark)
- Loss would be total revenue – total costs = £8,000 – £12,000 = loss of £4,000. (1 mark)

8. What might be the advantages and disadvantages for them of expanding their business to offer
kennels for overnight accommodation of pets? (9)

Indicative content

Advantages

- Increase income - possibly profit depending on costs.
- New markets of the business – can diversify to limit risk.
- Better marketing – word of mouth spreads about new service from existing customers.

Disadvantages

- Initial investment likely to be high – cost of buildings etc.
- Risk that new venture might fail – moving into unknown area – may not be demand for the new business.
- Borrowing to finance the investment - increase interest payments and costs.
- Time taken away from working on existing business - which could suffer.
- Would need to carry out research to find out if new business was profitable and if there was a market.

Mark scheme

Level	Mark	Descriptor
	No mark	Non-rewardable material
Level 1	1–3	At least one advantage and disadvantage stated with limited or no explanation. For example, 'They might make more profit but they could also fail.'
Level 2	4–6	At least one advantage and disadvantage stated with some explanation. For example, 'They might make more profit because they would be able to generate more revenue from extra sales. However, they could risk making a loss because it is a new market for them which they do not know very well.'
Level 3	7–9	At least one advantage and disadvantage stated with clear explanation and examples given. For example, 'This is a new market for Kevin and Emma and it brings possible costs and benefits. The new market might help them to spread their risks. Diversifying their business in this way mean that if one part of the business slows down the other might help them to maintain revenue. However, they are moving into a new area which they have little knowledge of. This is risky because they will be learning whilst doing the work and they could make a loss as a result of their lack of experience.'

Chapter 15: **Estimating revenues, costs and profits**

1   What is meant by the term 'turnover'?

2   What is meant by the term 'fixed costs'?

3   What is meant by the term 'variable costs'?

4   How is total cost calculated?

5   Explain the difference between the measurement of sales volume and sales revenue.

6   Explain the difference between cost and price.

Ivie Clarke has decided to launch a numbers game like Sudoku. She estimates her fixed costs to be £5,000. The variable costs are £1.20 per game. She intends to sell the games for £5.00 each. Ivie estimates she will sell 1,400 games a month.

7   (a) What is her total revenue if she sells 1,400 games?

   (b) What are her total costs if she sells 1,400 games?

   (c) How much profit does she make if she sells 1,400 games?

8   How many games does she need to sell to cover her total costs?

9   In fact the fixed costs of the business were actually £5,500. How much profit or loss would Ivie make if she sold 1,400 games?

10 State two reasons why Ivie's costs might be higher than she estimated.

Suggested answers

1 Turnover is the amount of income received by a business from selling its goods or services. It is also known as revenue or sales revenue.

2 Fixed costs are costs that are not dependent on the level of output.

3 Variable costs are costs that change directly with the number of products produced by the business.

4 Total costs (TC) are calculated by adding together fixed costs (FC) and variable costs (VC), i.e. TC = FC + VC.

5 Sales volume is measured in number of units, whilst sales revenue is measured in currency.

6 Cost is what the producer bears when making the product. Price is the amount of money the customer has to exchange for the product.

7 (a) Total revenue = 1,400 x £5.00 = £7,000.

   (b) Total costs are fixed costs of £5,000 + variable costs of £1.20 x 1,400 (1,680) = £6,680.

   (c) Profit = £7,000 - £6,680 = £320.

8   To cover all costs she needs to sell £6,680 ÷ £5.00 = 1,336 games.

9 She will make a loss of £180. Total revenue of £7,000 - total costs of (£5,500 + 1,680) = £7,000 - £7,180.

10 She might have underestimated costs such as insurance. She might have underestimated the cost of phone calls. Interest rates may have risen and this may have increased the cost of repayments on an overdraft or loan.

Chapter 16: **Forecasting cash flows**

1. A small bakery has just launched a new range of cakes. Which of the following is **not** a cash inflow for the small bakery business? Select **one** answer.

   A   Capital from the owner to help launch the range

   B   Buying ingredients for the cakes

   C   A loan to help launch the range

   D   Sales from the new range of cake

   Answer B

Comments
A Incorrect – if the owner puts money into a business, this is a cash inflow.
B Correct – money flows out of the business to buy ingredients, so this is not a cash inflow.
C Incorrect – a loan led to money flowing into the business, which is a cash inflow.
D Incorrect – selling the new range of cakes will earn the business cash, so this will be a cash inflow.

2. A business has produced a cash flow forecast for January.

   Total receipts of a business are £17,000.

   Total payments are £15,000.

   The opening balance is £10,000.

   What will be the net cash flow at the end of January? Select **one** answer.

   A   £10,000

   B   £12,000

   C   £2,000

   D   £32,000

   Answer C

Comments
A Incorrect – this is just the opening balance.
B Incorrect – this is an incorrect calculation by adding net cash flow to the opening balance.
C Correct – net cash flow is receipts - payments (£17,000 - £15,000 = £2,000).
D Incorrect – this is an incorrect calculation by adding total receipts to total payments.

3. The following table shows the cash flow forecast for business for three months of the year. Fill in the blanks.

£

	June	July	August
Total receipts	60,000	70,000	78,000
Payments			
Materials	20,000	30,000	42,000
Other costs	60,000	75,000	85,000
Total payments	80,000	105,000	127,000
Net cash flow	-20,000	-35,000	-49,000
Opening balance	30,000	10,000	-25,000
Closing balance	10,000	-25,000	-74,000

Materials in June (£20,000) = Total payments (£80,000) – Other costs (£60,000)

Total receipts in July (£70,000) = Total payments (£105,000) – Net cash flow (35,000)

Opening balance in July (£10,000) = Closing balance in June (£10,000)

Net cash flow in August (-£49,000) = Total receipts (£78,000) – Total payments (£127,000)

Chapter 16: Forecasting cash flows

Aziz Duah decided to set up a business selling printed t-shirts. He researched the market and found that there was no-one in the area offering this service. He thought that selling to businesses or to rock bands for their fans would be successful. Aziz would offer to design and print the t-shirts with their own designs. He would begin trading in September. His sales forecast included the following information.

Receipts

- September £14,000, October £15,000, November £18,500 and December £19,500

Payments

- Machinery and office equipment are £9,000 in September.

- Wages are £5,000 in September and October and £10,000 in November and December.

- Heating and lighting are £1,000 a quarter. The first payment is October.

- Other costs are £2,200 a month.

- Materials are £2,000 a month in September, October and November. In December Aziz plans to arrange a 30 day payment period for materials.

- Insurance is £3,500 for the year, payable in October.

- There is no opening cash balance.

Table 2 Cash flow forecast, first 4 months of trading

	Sept	Oct	Nov	Dec
			£	
Total receipts	14,000	15,000	18,500	19,500
Payments				
Machinery & equipment	9,000	0	0	0
Wages	5,000	5,000	10,000	10,000
Heating & lighting	0	1,000	0	0
Other costs	2,200	2,200	2,200	2,200
Materials	2,000	2,000	2,000	0
Insurance	0	3,500	0	0
Total payments	18,200	•••••	14,200	12,200
Net cash flow	•••••	1,300	4,300	•••••
Opening balance	0	-4,200	-2,900	1,400
Closing balance	-4,200	-2,900	•••••	8,700

1. Calculate the missing figures in the table. (4)

£

	Sept	Oct	Nov	Dec
Total receipts	14,000	15,000	18,500	19,500
Payments				
Machinery & equipment	9,000	0	0	0
Wages	5,000	5,000	10,000	10,000
Heating & lighting	0	1,000	0	0
Other costs	2,200	2,200	2,200	2,200
Materials	2,000	2,000	2,000	0
Insurance	0	3,500	0	0
Total payments	18,200	**13,700**	14,200	12,200
Net cash flow	**-4,200**	1,300	4,300	**7,300**
Opening balance	0	-4,200	-2,900	1,400
Closing balance	-4,200	-2,900	**1,400**	8,700

2. Analyse why the business has cash flow problem in September but not December. (6)

Indicative content

In September

Explain that in September outflows/total payments (£18,200) are more than inflows/total receipts (£14,000).

Explain why this is cash flow problem – there is more money leaving the business than coming in. There is a net cash flow of -£4,200

Analyse a reason for this, ie in September too much stock may have been bought

In December

Explain that in December inflows/total receipts (£19,500) are more than outflows/total payments (£12,200)

Explain why there is no cash flow problem – there is more money coming into the business than leaving. There is a net cash flow of £7,300.

Analyse a reason for this, ie trade terms have been agreed so that payments are delayed until the following month.

Mark scheme

Level	Mark	Descriptor
	No mark	Non-rewardable material
Level 1	1–2	The reason why a business has a cash flow problem will be stated but supported by limited examples and with no explanation.
Level 2	3–4	The reason why a business has a cash flow problem will be stated, supported by some good examples.
Level 3	5–6	The reason why a business has a cash flow problem will be clearly explained, supported by excellent examples.

3. Aziz is thinking of taking out a long-term bank loan to improve cash flow. Do you think he should do this? (6)

Indicative content

Some reasons why he might take out the loan might include:

- he will get the money immediately;
- he will have a long time to pay it off;
- the money will be guaranteed as it will be provided by a bank or other institution;
- it will probably be for the total amount he estimates he needs, providing he can convince the bank of the lack of risk in his business plan.

Some reasons why he might not take out the loan could include:

- he will have to pay interest on the loan as well as repaying the loan itself;
- interest could be high and would have to be paid back over a long period;
- the bank may set conditions on the loan;
- the bank might want collateral/security such as buildings or equipment, to be set against the loan.
- he may be able to get the cash flow from other sources which could be cheaper. These could include
  - putting more money into the business himself
  - asking others to put money into the business
  - find other ways increase revenue or reduce costs.
- many new businesses fail but he could still be liable for the loan.
- there is no evidence from the forecast that a long term loan is necessary.

As a general rule using a bank loan would have to be considered very carefully. A bank is likely to be reluctant to lend money simply to cover the cash flow as they might expect other methods to be tried first.

Mark scheme

Level	Mark	Descriptor
	No mark	Non-rewardable material
Level 1	1–2	A choice will be made with poorly developed justification and supported by limited examples.
Level 2	3–4	A choice will be made with some developed justification and supported by some good examples.
Level 3	5–6	A choice will be made with a clearly developed justification and supported by excellent examples.

Chapter 16: Forecasting cash flows

1   What is meant by the term 'cash flow'?

2   What is meant by the term 'inflows'?

3   List three examples of possible inflows to a business.

4   What is meant by the term 'outflows'?

5   List four examples of possible outflows from a business.

6   Define the term 'net cash flow'.

7   What is meant by the term 'cash flow forecast'?

8   State two reasons why a business might compile a cash flow forecast.

9   A business has receipts of £20,000 in January and payments of £15,000. What is the net cash flow in January?

10 A business in month one of trading has a net cash flow of - £2,000.

    (a) What is the value of payments if receipts are £4,000?

    (b) What is its closing balance if its opening balance was £3,500?

    (c) What is the opening balance in month two?

Suggested answers

1 Cash flow is the money going into and out of a business over a period of time.

2 Inflows are the cash flowing into the business. These are sometimes called receipts.

3 Inflows include owners' capital, bank loans, cash from selling the products and shareholders' investment.

4 Outflows are the cash flowing out of the business. These are sometimes called payments.

5 Outflows might be wages, advertising costs, electricity and gas payments, interest paid on loans, accountant's fees, payments for raw materials or maintenance of equipment.

6 The receipts (inflows) to a business minus the payments (outflows).

7 A prediction or estimate or educated guess about receipts and payments into and out of a business over time.

8 A business might compile a cash flow forecast to see if it is likely to make a profit before it starts trading. If not then it will not start. It could also use it to help get a loan from the bank. Most importantly, it uses the forecast to check whether the actual cash flow is the same as the forecast. If it is worse then the business can do something about the problem.

9 The net cash flow is £20,000 - £15,000 = £5,000.

10 (a) Payments are £6,000. If net cash flow is minus £2,000 then payments must be £2,000 more than receipts (which are £4,000).

(b) The closing balance is £1,500. This is the opening balance of £3,500 minus the net cash flow of £2,000 (£3,500 - £2,000) = £1,500.

(c) The opening balance next month is £1,500 as it is the same as the closing balance from the previous month.

Chapter 17: **The business plan**

1. Which three of the following would a start-up business be **most likely** to include in its business plan?

   Select **three** answers.

   A   A cash flow forecast

   B   A photograph of the business owners

   C   The location of the business

   D   How the product will be marketed

   E   The names of all its past customers

   F   The names of all its past suppliers

   G   The names and addresses of all employees

   Answer A, C and D

Comments
A Correct – a cash flow forecast would help a business plan its future performance.
B Incorrect – a photograph of the business' owners would be unlikely to provide any real help towards the planning of the business.
C Correct – the location of the business would be an important feature for planning and the performance of the business.
D Correct – how the product will be marketed would be an important feature for planning and the performance of the business.
E Incorrect – the names of all its past customers would not be included as a new business would not have past customers and the names of customers would not help a current business plan its future performance.
F Incorrect – he names of all its past suppliers would not be included as a new business would not have past suppliers and the names of suppliers would not help a current business plan its future performance.
G Incorrect – the names and addresses of all employees are too much detail to be included in a business plan.

2. Which two of the following are **most likely** to be the reasons why the owners of a start-up business would draw up a business plan?

   Select **two** answers.

   A   To minimise the risks associated with starting a business.

   B   To persuade a bank to lend money to the business.

   C   To prove to Her Majesty's Revenue and Customs that the right amount of tax is being paid.

   D   To calculate the profit from the operations of the business to date.

   E   To reduce the rent on the premises which the business is using

Answer A and B

Comments
A Correct – a business plan would help to reduce the risks associated with starting a business.
B Correct – a business plan would help to persuade a bank to lend money to the business.
C Incorrect – this is not the correct document to prove to Her Majesty's Revenue and Customs that the right amount of tax is being paid.
D Incorrect – this is not the correct document to calculate the profit from the operations of the business to date.
E Incorrect – a business plan would not help to reduce the rent on the premises which the business is using.

3. Drawing up a business plan helps reduce the risks of starting a business because

 A banks like to see a business plan

 B every business has a business plan

 C a business plan encourages the entrepreneur to think about all aspects of the business

 D profits can only be made if a business plan has been drawn up

Select **one** answer.

Answer C

Comments
A Incorrect – this would not help to reduce risk.
B Incorrect – not every business has a business plan, even if every business did have a business plan it would not, in itself, reduce risk – it depends how good the plan is.
C Correct – thinking about all aspects of the business may help to reduce risk.
D Incorrect – this would not reduce risk. A business plan could help a business to make profit but it is not guaranteed to do so.

Chapter 17: The business plan

Kenton Travel Ltd was set up in 2009. It managed to achieve its first business aim, to make a profit of £5,000, in the first year. Kenton Travel is owned by Mohammad Ashraful and Atiur Rahman. The travel company provides small group tours to places like Vietnam, Cambodia and Indonesia.

Both Mohammad and Atiur are experienced travellers and wanted to mix business with pleasure when they first decided to start a business. They are both actively involved in leading tours and thoroughly enjoy what they do. Indeed, their success in business is partly down to their passion for travel that rubs off on their small group customers. However, planning before they started trading was also an important ingredient. The pair spent nearly two years researching destinations, accommodation, modes of travel and routes before drawing up a comprehensive business plan. They also went on courses to learn about marketing and accounting.

When Mohammad and Atiur drew up their cash flow forecast, they included the cost of setting up a website and advertising regularly in Sunday newspapers. They predicted that customers would spend an average of £3,000 each. In their cash flow forecast, they put in high figures for their costs and low figures for the sales. They hoped that making very cautious estimates would minimise the risk of their business failing within the first year due to lack of cash.

1. (a) What is meant by the term 'business plan'? (1)

Indicative content

A business plan is a plan for the development of a business including forecasts. It is finance-based with qualitative evidence to support it. It helps to reduce risk by thinking ahead.

Mark scheme
1 mark for an appreciation of at least one of the elements in the definition above.

(b) Give **three** examples of things that Mohammed and Atiur would have included in their business plan. (3)

Indicative content

* Projected income – number of customers x £3,000 (their average spending)

* Expenses – advertising costs, website maintenance, rent

* The nature of the business activity — a travel company provides small group tours to places like Vietnam, Cambodia and Indonesia

* The key personnel of the business – Mohammad Ashraful and Atiur Rahman who would run the business themselves.

Mark scheme
1 mark for each appropriate example.

2.   Explain **two** ways in which Mohammad and Atiur did research which helped them to write their business plan before trading began.   (8)

Indicative content

- Did tour – leading to experience of how to run such as business and what competitors may do – help the business be competitive against rivals and survive the first year of trading.

- Researched marketing and accounting – knowledge of how to promote the business and financial control – help to make a profit (maximise revenue and minimise costs).

Mark scheme

1 mark for each way identified and up to 3 marks for the explanation for each. For the full three marks the explanation will clearly show links between the way and how it helped the pair draw up their business plan. For example, The two did some market research (1 mark for the way) which helped them to understand their market (1 mark). This told them whether there would be enough customers of their business (1 mark) which they could have used to develop revenue forecasts for their plan (1 mark).

For 2 marks, the explanation is simplistic, for example, They did market research (1 mark). This would tell them whether anyone would buy their product. (1 mark)

3.   Mohammad and Atiur had a 'passion' for their business and drew up a business plan before they started. In your opinion would this help to get rid of all the risks of setting up a new business? Justify your answer.   (8)

Indicative content

- Business plan should show a business what it is trying to achieve and whether this is realistic – this can help reduce risk.

- Business plan could highlight problems which could be prevented before they take place – if the problems are too high then the pair could abandon the idea before committing too much money.

- Always a risk not matter how good a plan is.

- Political situations at destinations could be external factor which it is not possible to predict in a plan.

- The plan might highlight that the target market might be limited – this might persuade them to drop the idea before they spend too much.

- Building caution into the plan is good, but still only an estimate – their estimates could be wrong

Mark scheme

Level	Mark	Descriptor
	No mark	Non-rewardable material
Level 1	1–2	A choice will be made with poorly developed justification and supported by limited examples. For example, 'No it would not because it is only a plan not real.'
Level 2	3–5	A choice will be made with some developed justification and supported by some good examples. There will be some balance to the answer. For example, 'Planning can help to take into account many things. They can estimate cash flow, set budgets, include market research and thinking about these things helps reduce the risk. However, there will always be some risk so the answer is, no.'
Level 3	6–8	A choice will be made with a clearly developed justification and supported by excellent examples. There will be a clear balance in the answer. Appropriate terminology will be used and there is likely to be a clear conclusion drawn at the top end of the band. For example, a business plan helps a business consider things that will affect their business. Market research can tell the business what their market might be and enable them to estimate their revenue. This allows them to produce a cash flow forecast which helps to tell them whether the business will work. But even if they plan really carefully there is always a risk that the business might fail. Their estimates could be inaccurate and things can happen outside their control like a rise in interest rates. As a result, no business plan can get rid of all risks.'

Chapter 17: **The business plan**

1   What is a business plan?

2   State four non-financial items that would appear on a business plan.

3   State four financial items that would appear on a business plan.

4   What is meant by the term 'forecasting' in relation to sales and costs?

5   What might be included under the heading 'key personnel' in a business plan?

6   State two examples of key personnel in a restaurant.

7   State a possible aim that a costume hiring business might have.

8   Explain how a business could use its business plan once it has started trading.

9   Explain why a new business with a business plan is more likely to succeed than a business which does not have a plan.

10 State two reasons why a bank manager would want to see a business plan before endorsing a loan.

Suggested answers

1   A business plan is a plan for the development of the business.

2   Four non-financial items might be location, suppliers, personnel, production methods, marketing plan and ownership type.

3   Four financial items might be variable costs, fixed costs, rent, raw materials, utilities, wages, advertising, total costs, total revenue and cash flow.

4   This is an educated attempt to guess what the sales and costs are likely to be based on research carried out.

5   These are the main employees of the business.

6   Examples of key personnel in a restaurant might be the head chef and the manager.

7   To provide a wide variety of costumes and an excellent service for customers and become the number one choice for costume hire in the area.

8   A business would use its business plan as a monitoring tool so that it could check its actual performance against its forecast. This would tell it whether the research was accurate, insufficient or wrong. It would indicate where under- or over-estimation had taken place.

9   A business which has a business plan might be better able to spot when problems might arise, e.g. cash flow problems, and be able to do something about them before they become too big to solve. Without a plan a business may not be able to identify and anticipate these problems, which could lead to failure.

10 A bank manager would like to see a business plan for several reasons. It would show how keen and interested the parties were. It would show how good they were at investigating the business. Further, it would indicate whether it was worth backing. Also, the bank could compare it with similar ones to see if it made business sense.

Chapter 18: **Obtaining finance**

1. Which two of the following are examples of long-term finance for a high street chain of fashion shops?

   Select **two** answers.

   A   An overdraft

   B   Trade credit

   C   A three-year bank loan

   D   New shares

   E   A Christmas sale

   Answer C and D

Comments
A Incorrect – an overdraft is a short-term source of finance.
B Incorrect – trade credit is a short-term source of finance.
C Correct – a three-year bank loan is a long-term source of finance.
D Correct – new shares are a long-term source of finance.
E Incorrect – a Christmas sale is a short-term source of finance.

2. On which one of the following would a business pay interest?

   Select **one** answer.

   A   An overdraft

   B   A share

   C   Personal savings

   D   Retained profit

   Answer A

Comments
A Correct – a business would pay interest to a bank on a bank loan as this is borrowed money.
B Incorrect – a business would pay a dividend on shares to shareholders.
C Incorrect – a business would not pay interest on savings, but it might be paid interest if these were savings in a bank account.
D Incorrect – this is money made in previous years held within the business. It does not pay interest on this as it is not money that is borrowed.

3. Which **one** of the following is most likely to be an example of a type of finance where the lender can demand immediate repayment from a business which has borrowed the money?

    Select **one** answer.

    A   An overdraft

    B   A share

    C   A bank loan

    D   Retained profit

    Answer A

Comments
A Correct – a bank can demand immediate repayment on an overdraft.
B Incorrect – a business does not have to repay money invested in it by buying shares.
C Incorrect – a bank loan is usually repaid after a fixed and agreed period.
D Incorrect – a business keeps this within the business.

Chapter 18: Obtaining finance

Perth Holdings Ltd is a Scottish-based company that makes drilling and other engineering equipment for the oil industry. It was set up in 2001 with £160 000 of share capital, a £40 000 bank loan and a £10 000 local authority grant. The shares were owned equally by Ella McDonald and Shane MacTaggart. Ella, who studied Business at Glasgow University, insisted that the business should be properly funded at the start. She knew that small businesses that lacked funding in the initial stages often struggled. The company rents a factory unit on an industrial estate and leases about 80 per cent of its machinery and equipment.

The company has done well since starting up. The rising oil price has resulted in a boom in oil exploration and Perth Holdings has benefited. Most of the company's recent growth has been funded through retained profit. This has avoided the need to increase the amount borrowed through loans significantly.

In 2008, the price of oil reached a record high and the factory was running at full capacity. Ella and Shane decided it was time to move to larger premises and cash in on the continuing boom. They drew up a business plan for expansion. They calculated they would need to raise £200 000 to make the move and update their technology. A bank agreed to loan them all the money.

1. Analyse **two** differences between 'share capital' and a 'bank loan'. (6)

Indicative content

Share capital

- Gives part ownership.
- Not returnable/repayable as a sum.
- Risk is by investor.
- Only the shares can be sold.
- Owners entitled to a share of profits.

Loan

- Usually secured against an asset.
- Repayable usually over a fixed term.
- Bank has no ownership in business.
- Interest charged.

Mark scheme

Level	Mark	Descriptor
	No mark	Non-rewardable material
Level 1	1–2	Simple statement with no/limited supporting explanation. For example, 'A share is where someone owns part of the business, a bank loan is not'.
Level 2	3–6	Two differences stated with some explanation. For example, 'Share capital is money that is invested by shareholders and gives them part ownership in the business. An investor making a loan to a business does not own any part of the business but expects their money to be repaid at some agreed time in the future with interest'. This would be worth 3 marks.

2. Explain **two** reasons why a company like Perth Holdings would choose to lease machinery and equipment rather than buying it outright. (6)

Indicative content

- Not burdened with selling it at the end.
- Known regular financial outlay.
- Avoids capital being tied up at start – better cash flow initially.
- Maintenance problems sorted by leasing company.

Mark scheme

Level	Mark	Descriptor
	No mark	Non-rewardable material
Level 1	1–2	Up to two examples will be stated.
Level 2	3–4	Up to two examples will be stated with limited explanation.
Level 2	5–6	Up to two examples will be stated with good explanation.

3. Perth Holdings Ltd could borrow the £200,000 from a bank or seek investment from a venture capitalist to help it expand. In your opinion, which would be the better option for Perth Holdings Ltd to fund its expansion? (8)

Indicative content

Bank

- Known source.
- Simple – no hidden agenda.
- Fixed repayments – but must be repaid.
- No controlling interests.

Venture capital

- Speculative.
- May have hidden costs.
- Have own agenda which may not be the same as the business.
- Can pull out at any time.

Mark scheme

Level	Mark	Descriptor
	No mark	Non-rewardable material
Level 1	1–2	A choice will be made with poorly developed justification and supported by limited examples. For example, 'Get the money from a bank because you get the money straight away.'
Level 2	3–5	A choice will be made with some developed justification and supported by some good examples. For example, 'Money gained from a venture capitalist means the business has to give up some of its control of the business but in return they get access to funds and the expertise of the venture capitalist'.
Level 3	6–8	A choice will be made with a clearly developed justification and supported by excellent examples. For example, 'A bank loan would be better for Perth Holdings Ltd because they will not lose any control of the business as they would if they used a venture capitalist. They will know what the length of the agreement is and what the interest payments are. Venture capitalists are investing to make a profit and this may mean that the venture capitalist has a different view about how the business is run to Ella and Shane. A bank will not interfere in this way if they agree to the loan.

Chapter 18: **Obtaining finance**

1   What is meant by the term 'short-term' finance?

2   What is meant by the term 'long-term' finance'?

3   What is meant by the term 'security' when obtaining finance?

4   What are grants?

5   What is meant by the term 'overdraft'?

Winona Talon decided to open a business making bases for flower arranging. She needed a small factory for production.

6   Why might Winona use a mortgage to buy the factory?

7   Why could the business not make use of retained profit as a source of finance?

A clothing retailer needed money quickly as it had cash flow problems. It sold its debts of £80,000 to Fastcash Factors which paid 90% of invoice values.

8   Explain how factoring can help the clothing retailer.

9   How much would the clothing retailer have received from the factor?

10 How could the clothing retailer have used trade credit from suppliers to help its cash flow problem?

Suggested answers

1 Sources of money that are invested or borrowed for less than a year.

2 Sources of money that are invested or borrowed for more than a year.

3 Security is the value of assets, e.g. a factory, that a business 'puts up' to guarantee a loan, so if it fails to pay back the loan the assets can be sold to obtain the money for the lender.

4 Grants are money paid out by government organisations or charities to businesses. They are given to businesses that need help for particular reasons, for example when they first set up.

5 An overdraft is the borrowing of money by a business that involves taking out more from a current account at a bank than is actually in the account. Interest is paid on the amount overdrawn and a limit is usually agreed on the amount which can be overdrawn.

6 A mortgage would be used as this source of finance is designed for the purchase of property. The business is given money to buy premises and their value is used as security in case the loan cannot be repaid. As the money is loaned over a long period of time, the repayments per month are lower.

7 Retained profit is money built up in a business from profit in previous years. A new business such as this would not have any retained profit to use, therefore...

8 Factoring involves a company called a 'factor' buying the debt of another business that has a cash flow problem. The factor company only pays a percentage of what is owed to the original business. The original business gets an injection of cash and the factor company makes a profit by collecting the full amount owed in the first place, but has to wait for it.

9 The clothing retailer received £72,000 (£80,000 x 90%)

10 Trade credit is where goods are received now and paid for later. The clothing retailer could have delayed its payments to suppliers. This would have meant that cash was taken out of the business at a later date, leaving the retailer with more cash in months when it might have a problem.

Practice exam questions

> Anne Milford knew from her work in the fashion world that there was a demand for up-market hampers for glamorous picnics and parties. Even though she had been involved in this type of business, she felt her contacts would give her the start she needed.
>
> She did some research locally and found there were no competitors. However, she did not carry out in-depth research about sales beyond her contacts. She was not aware of sales trends, what prices were charged or even whether such businesses existed. She believed the quality of the product, her reputation, determination, self-belief and word of mouth would be enough to generate sales and meet her objectives of being rich and famous. She had £20,000 of her own to start the business, which she would run from the house that she owned in Sunderland. Other than some utility bills, such as gas, electricity, telephone and water, accountants' fees and raw material costs, Anne thought she would have no other overheads. This led her to believe the objective of being rich would happen relatively easily.
>
> From her research Anne knew that she would need some extra finance to start her business. She asked her friends Toni and Linda if they would like to invest. They looked at the ideas which she had set out in a business plan. As a result of looking at the plan they decided not to invest. Anne turned to her bank, as her personal savings were not enough. The bank told her that her business plan was not detailed enough and that she needed to think about her financial projections more carefully. They also wanted to see a cash flow forecast and some budgets. Anne had been happier drawing up the marketing part of the plan than the financial part.

(a) Which **two** of the following costs will Anne **not** have to pay? (2)

   A   Staff wages

   B   Raw materials

   C   Electricity

   D   Rent

   E   Heating

   F   Water

Answer A and D

Examiner's comment
A Correct – staff wages will not have to be paid as she will not be employing anyone.
B Incorrect – raw materials will have to be paid as she will have to buy raw materials to make the hampers.
C Incorrect – electricity charges will have to be paid as she will have to pay utility bills.
D Correct – rent will not have to be paid as she will be working from her own home.
E Incorrect – heating charges will have to be paid as she will have to pay to heat the house.
F Incorrect – water rates have to be paid and as a business she is bound to use water.

(b) Anne sees herself as an entrepreneur. Describe **two** qualities she will need to succeed in her business venture. (4)

Indicative content

- Been successful once in tough career area
- Determined
- No competition
- Not distracted by outside pressure, e.g. social life

Mark scheme

Two appropriate qualities are identified (1 mark for each) along with some description of how this quality will help her succeed. For example, 'She is a determined character because she has decided to follow a completely new career.' or 'She has asked for help from the bank in case things don't go to plan; she is thinking ahead.'

(c) Do you think that you would invest in Anne's business? Justify your answer. (6)

Indicative content

Reasons not to invest

- Nothing about level of sales
- No prices
- No hard research only gut reaction
- No experience
- Business plan not detailed enough - especially in the financial planning area

Reasons to invest

- No competition
- Few overheads so profit could be large
- Knows right people
- She's determined

Mark scheme

Level	Mark	Descriptor
	No mark	Non-rewardable material
Level 1	1–2	Judgement about why will be given, but there will be little or no support for the statement, for example 'I would not invest because I think her business will not succeed.'
Level 2	3–4	Judgement is given along with some developed support. This will be drawn from the passage. For example, 'I would not invest in Anne's business. I do not think that Anne has thought enough about the business. Her business plan was not detailed enough and does not have enough financial information.'
Level 3	5–6	Judgement is given with well-developed support that draws on the passage and also uses appropriate terminology. For example, 'I would not invest in a business that had not been thought through carefully. I think that this is the case with Anne's business. She has not carried out enough in-depth research. The bank pointed out to Anne that she did not have enough financial details. Linda and Tony did not invest, which might indicate that they saw problems as well. I would want to see a cash flow forecast at least before deciding whether the risk was worth it and Anne does not have this.'

Case study

Jason Livermore had worked in sports centres for a number of years. At 28 he was feeling frustrated and wanted to take on more responsibility. He noticed that at certain times of the day a certain type of customer visited the centres. They were either parents who looked after children or business people who appeared to have limited time. He talked to these customers and found that they would like a personal trainer who could tailor fitness programmes to their needs.

That was four years ago. He set up his own business having rented rooms in a town centre and operated as a fitness centre specialising in offering tailor made personal fitness programmes. The marketing mix for the new business was simple. He charged a competitive price for his programmes compared to local sports and fitness centres. His promotion strategy was to maintain contact with customers through phone calls and emails. At regular intervals he would meet with his customers to check that the programme was to their satisfaction. At the same time, he would ask whether there were any other people they knew who would be interested in his services. As for 'place' in the marketing mix, he dealt directly with customers who were all in the local area, within 15 miles of his centre.

For the first couple of years, Jason operated as a sole trader. As the number of customers expanded he moved to new premises. Having taken advice, Jason decided to set up change the ownership and become a private limited company to reduce risks should the business not do well in the future. By this stage, he was employing four workers and had registered to pay VAT 6 months previously. His company was now responsible for paying VAT, National Insurance contributions and corporation tax. He and his workers also paid income tax.

Two years further on and Jason bought new machinery because of the demand for his services. He also expanded the services to include lifestyle advice and yoga. He put his success down to excellent customer service. His programmes suited his customers' needs. He knew his customers were satisfied because of the amount of repeat business he did. Nearly all customers renewed their membership each year.

Buying the new machines meant recruiting more staff. With skilled workers in short supply, he did not get many applications from his adverts. He was also aware that he wanted to recruit staff that would be well motivated and have a positive attitude to work.

Dealing with all the legal aspects of running a business was difficult. For a start, there was all the employment legislation relating to discrimination, recruitment and redundancy. However, he felt that, if he treated his staff fairly, they would be well motivated and he would keep within the law.

Suggested discussion points/answers

1. Explain why customers and customer satisfaction are so important for Jason's business.

- No customers, no business
- Repeat business
- Reputation
- Cheap advertising
- Word of mouth
- Easy business/people come to him
- Very specific target market
- Health

2. Why does setting up a private limited company reduce risk compared to operating as a sole trader?

- Personal finance/assets same as business' finance
- Could lose everything he owned (house, car) as a sole trader – now has limited liability
- As a sole trader he might have to declare bankruptcy if the business failed
- Only lose amount of money invested under limited liability
- Could start another business if did he not lose everything.

3. What could be the problems for Jason's business if his staff were **not** well motivated?

- Lose customers

- Bad impression

- Bad reputation – hard to regain

- Lose business altogether

- Might have to leave industry

- Insolvent

4. Should Jason spend more on promoting his business to customers? Justify your answer.

Yes

- May have spare capacity

- Gain wider market

- More profit

No

- Cost

- Current 'promotion' is nearly free

- May take up his time/take him away from his main role

- May have to use other services for promotion

- Customers already satisfied

- May not want to expand too quickly

_____

Chapter 19: Customer focus and the marketing mix

1. Which **two** of the following would be essential elements of customer focus for a business?

   Select **two** answers.

   A   Anticipating customer needs

   B   Ordering stocks of raw materials

   C   Meeting customer needs

   D   Paying consumer tax

   E   Paying workers

   Answer A and C

Comments
A Correct – customer focus includes attempts to predict what consumers might want or need.
B Incorrect – this is to do with suppliers not customers.
C Correct – all businesses must supply what is needed by consumers or they will not survive.
D Incorrect – there is no such thing as consumer tax – this is a red herring.
E Incorrect – this is a cost not a part of the customer focus.

2. Which **two** of the following would be part of the marketing mix for a business?

   Select **two** answers.

   A   Production

   B   Place

   C   Stocks

   D   Price

   E   Workers

   Answer B and D

Comments
A Incorrect – this is about how the product is made.
B Correct – this is about how the product is made available to the consumer.
C Incorrect – this is what the business keeps to meet supply.
D Correct – this is what the business tells the customer they will have to give up in order to acquire the product.
E Incorrect – workers make the product and are not what the business sells.

3. Which **two** of the following would be the **most likely** examples of promotion?

   Select **two** answers.

   A   Stocks

   B   Two for one offers

   C   Production

   D   Quality

   E   Advertising

   Answer B and E

Comments
A Incorrect – this is what the business holds to meet supply.
B Correct – this is enticing the customer to buy the product.
C Incorrect – this is about the method of making the product.
D Incorrect – this is to do with the product.
E Correct – this is one way in which the business informs its customers.

Chapter 19: Customer focus and the marketing mix

Hannah works in the design department for a designer clothes manufacturing business. However, she has plans to set up her own business. The business will manufacture clothes specially designed by Hannah for women aged 20-40 years who are sized 16 and above. Hannah's friends and family have always told her how frustrated they are that so many fashion shops do not stock larger sizes for fashion conscious women. They said 'You should really do something about this'. She wants her clothes to be exciting, fashionable but reasonably priced. Her range will include pieces suitable to wear to go to work at the office, or for a night out with friends.

Working for an existing business, Hannah knows that one of her biggest problems will be persuading shops to buy her collection of clothes. If she cannot get her clothes into shops, she will not be able to get her 20–40 year old target market to buy her clothes. Setting up a website to sell directly to customers is one way round the problem. However, this probably will not give enough sales to make her business a success. She will have to persuade shops and boutiques to stock her clothes. To do this, she will have to take a stand at the regular trade fairs that are visited by the owners of independent clothes retailers where they choose and buy their stock. Promotion would also mean sending out brochures and leaflets to shops that might consider buying her products. Advertisements in selected magazines might also be affordable.

1. Explain how each **one** of the following elements of the marketing mix could contribute to the success of Hannah's future business:

    (a) price   (3)

    (b) product   (3)

    (c) promotion   (3)

    (d) place.   (3)

Indicative content

Price

- Competitive
- Allow for store mark-up (profit)
- Cover costs
- Discount/bulk purchase
- Get buyers interested
- Recover investment

Product

- Quality
- Value for Money
- Fashion
- Flexibility – make to order if needed

Promotion

- Must decide on target market
- Shops or direct?
- Trade fairs – dedicated target audience
- Brochures – less effective
- Needs personal approach
- Models/video

Place

- Shops
- Distribution
- Availability via wide range of outlets
- Impulse buying
- Must match quality of product

Mark scheme

For each element of the marketing mix (a-d), up to 3 marks for a suitable explanation of how this element could contribute to the success of Hannah's future business. For example, 'The price Hannah sets can influence her future sales. (1 mark) The price she sets must be high enough to at least cover costs and let her make some profit. (1 mark) But she must set the price low enough to persuade shops to buy her collection of clothes.' (1 mark)

2. (i) What is meant by 'customer focus'? (1)

Indicative content

Customer focus means identifying, anticipating and meeting the needs of potential customers of the business.

Mark scheme

I mark for a suitable definition.

(ii) Explain why customer focus will be important to Hannah's business. (3)

Indicative content

- No customers, no business
- Awareness of what's needed
- Not established name so need to meet demand
- Need distribution bases, i.e. specialist buyers
- Need shop selling support
- Feedback about changes in market demand

Mark scheme

Up to 3 marks for a suitable explanation of why customer focus will be important to Hannah's business. For example, 'Identifying, anticipating and meeting the needs of customers effectively could help to make Hannah's business successful. (1 mark) Hannah is targeting a part of the market with very particular needs for women aged 20-40 years who are sized 16 and above. She also wants to offer a variety of styles, including work and day wear. (1 mark) If she does not meet the needs of this target market, she may be left with products that cannot be sold to any other group of women. Low sales and the high costs associated with unsold stock could make the business unprofitable. (1 mark)

3. 'The marketing mix for a shop which sold fashion clothes in larger sizes would be very different from the marketing mix for Hannah's business.' Do you agree with this? Justify your answer. (6)

Indicative content

Product

- Sell larger sizes (Hannah)
- Sell larger sizes, but may sell other sizes as well (Shops)

Price

- Competitive to get into shops/depends on prices shops will pay (Hannah)
- Can vary prices depending on demand/depends on prices that customers will pay (Shops)

Promotion

- To customers online/to retailers using brochures and leaflets/using trade fairs (Hannah)
- To customers online/to in magazines, other media – radio, television (Shops).

Place

- Through retailers, online (Hannah)
- In shops, online (Shops)

Mark scheme

Level	Mark	Descriptor
	No mark	Non-rewardable material
Level 1	1–2	A choice will be made with limited justification and supported by limited examples. For example, 'Yes. They will have different customers.'
Level 2	3–4	A choice will be made with some developed justification and supported by some good examples. 'Yes. Although there are some similarities, such as selling online, there are also differences. They have different customers with different needs. Manufacturers sell to shops, but retailers sell to customers. So the prices, products, promotion and distribution are likely to be different to some extent.'
Level 3	5–6	A choice will be made with a clearly developed justification and balance, supported by excellent examples. For example, 'There are likely to be some similarities in the marketing mix as they are both selling clothes. They are both targeting women, selling online and they must both set prices which are competitive. However, elements of the marketing mix may be different for a manufacturer and a retailer. For example, promotion may be different. They will both advertise, but the places they advertise, may be different. Shops may use television advertising and consumer magazines. Hannah may use leaflets and brochures for shop buyers and take products to trade fairs. The places they sell may also be different. Retailers will sell through shops. Hannah may sell directly to buyers. She will not have any shops.'

Chapter 19: Customer focus and the marketing mix

1   Give a definition of the term 'marketing'

2   What is meant by the term 'marketing mix'?

3   What is meant by the term 'price'?

4   What is meant by the term 'promotion'?

5   What is meant by the term 'place'?

6   Explain the term 'anticipating customer needs'.

7   Explain two ways that a business could identify customer needs.

Fenella Hiddiart is a qualified osteopath. She runs a business helping people back to health when they have muscle problems. It has the latest equipment and individual programs are designed for each person. Treatment takes place in a state of the art health centre. It deals with lots of sportspeople. She is keen to expand her business into other areas.

8   Explain why Fenella could charge a high price for her services.

9   Explain why Fenella might be more likely to advertise in a health magazine rather than a music magazine for customers.

10 Explain one service that Fenella could offer to move into other areas.

Suggested answers

1   Marketing is the process which seeks to anticipate, identify and satisfy customer needs profitably.

2   A combination of the factors of marketing combined in an appropriate way so each element is suited to the rest in order to aid the selling of a product. It consists of four main elements, price, promotion, product and place.

3   This is the amount of money the customer has to hand over in exchange for the product.

4   This is how the business communicates with the customer to raise awareness of the existence of the product and to create an image in the customer's mind about the product and what it will do.

5   This is how the business arranges for the customer to get the product, how it is distributed and how it gets to the end customer. It could be via a shop and home delivery for example.

6   This is where the business tries to find out about its customers' needs and is aware of its customers and its market, so that it is in a better position to be able to make sure the business meets those needs. It needs to be aware when fashions are changing and to changes its product(s) to meet that change before it is too late or before another business takes its customers.

7   The business could carry out market research to find out what customers want. It could produce some prototype products and see which suited the customers best before launching fully.

8   Fenella could charge a high price because her service is a luxury so users would expect to pay a high price. In their mind, the customers would associate high price with better quality, i.e. the image created by the product (a service in this case). If the price were too low, customers might think the service would not represent value for money.

9   She might advertise in a health magazine because her target market would be more likely to read that sort of magazine. They would have an interest in anything health-based so her promotion is likely to be effective. The readers of the health magazine are more likely to try her service than are the readers of the music magazine.

10 Fenella could adapt what she offers by branching into other health areas such as nutrition. If she gives customers a good service with her osteopathy they are more likely to accept her advice on healthy food. This could help the business to expand and increase turnover and profit.

Chapter 20: The importance of limited liability

1. A shareholder in a private limited company has

   A   unlimited liability

   B   an entitlement to a share of the profits of the company

   C   complete control of the company

   D   complete privacy about the financial affairs of the company

   Select **one** answer.

   Answer B

Comments
A Incorrect – unlimited liability is something a sole trader has.
B Correct – the shareholder invests to get a share of the profits.
C Incorrect – they only control a part depending on how many shares are owned.
D Incorrect – a private limited company must submit accounts to Companies House.

2. A sole trader faces more risk than a shareholder in a company because of

   A   changes in profits

   B   lack of control of the business

   C   unlimited liability

   D   lack of privacy

   Select **one** answer.

   Answer C

Comments
A Incorrect – this affects both types of ownership.
B Incorrect – the sole trader has more control.
C Correct – this is a feature of being a sole trader.
D Incorrect – this is not a risk.

3. Alfie Parkes is a sole trader who works as a gardener. His business has performed very poorly and it has run up debts of £50,000. Alfie has invested £75,000 in the business overall and has used his house as security for a loan of £30,000. His house is worth £200,000. He owes £20,000 to suppliers. How much of the debts run up by his business is Alfie responsible for paying himself if the business were to close?

Select **one** answer.

A   £20,000

B   £50,000

C   £75,000

D   £30,000

Answer B

Comments
A Incorrect – this is just part of the total debt.
B Correct – the business debts are also his personal debts.
C Incorrect – the debt is not £75,000 – that is how much he has invested, but if the business did close he risks losing this money.
D Incorrect – this is only part of the debt.

Chapter 20: The importance of limited liability

Edward and Reece Westwick, two brothers, worked for a number of building companies before deciding to set up their own business as scaffolders. Health and safety laws today mean that scaffolding is needed for most building jobs above first floor height level. So they expected to get plenty of work from builders needing scaffolding to be put up.

They have to decide what type of business they would form. Edward was the older brother and had more experience. They could have agreed to set up as a sole trader with Edward as the owner and Reece as an employee. However, Reece was not keen on simply being an employee. He wanted to be the joint owner of a business. So they are probably going to set up a private limited company. They would both be shareholders, owning half the company each. Setting up a private limited company would also have the advantage that it would reduce risks if the business did not do as well as they hoped.

1. Explain, using the Westwick brothers as an example, what is meant by (a) limited companies and (b) shareholders. (6)

Indicative content

(a)

- Limited liability
- Less risky
- Personal assets safe
- Shareholders (Edward and Reece)
- Owners and business seen as legally separate
- Only risk cash invested (50/50 here)
- File accounts

(b)

- Percentage of shares owned (50% each here)
- Part ownership (50/50 here)
- Share of profits (50/50 here)
- Shared control on decisions (50/50 here)
- Shared risks/liability (value of investment)

Mark scheme

Up to 3 marks for each application to Westwick brothers. For example, Shareholders are the joint owners of limited companies. (1 mark) Edward and Reece Westwick would be the shareholders if they set up a private limited company. Each would own a part or share of the business. (1 mark) In this case they agreed to own half the company (50 per cent) each. (1 mark) or Limited liability is when shareholders of a company are not personally liable for the debts of the company. (1 mark) If Edward and Reece Westwick set up a limited company and became shareholders they would each have limited liability. (1 mark) The most they can lose is the value of their investment in the shares if the company went out of business. (1 mark)

2. Why might setting up a limited company reduce risks for the two brothers? (3)

Indicative content

- If business fails only lose money invested, not personal belongings
- If one leaves the other does not inherit the liability
- Can walk away and only lose the amount invested, other debts 'die'
- Less risky
- Less likely to fall out
- Seems more professional, if needing bank support

Mark scheme

Up to 3 marks for an explanation of how a limited company reduces risks for the business. For example, Setting up a limited company means that shareholders, who are the owners of the business have limited liability. (1 mark) If business fails, then Edward and Reece who are the shareholders will only lose money invested, not their personal belongings. (1 mark) They can walk away from the business even if debts are unpaid or if one person leaves they do not have the liability of the business. (1 mark)

3. Consider **two** possible advantages for the two brothers of Edward becoming a sole trader and employing Reece, rather than setting up a limited company and both being shareholders. (6)

Indicative content

Sole trader	Limited company
Control all with Edward	50/50 control
Decisions made more quickly	Slows down decisions
Liability high for Edward (worse)	Liability 50% for Edward (better)
Liability nil for Reece (better)	Liability 50% for Reece (worse)
Edward gets all the profit	Edward gets 50% of profit
Reece gets a wage (could be > profit)	Reece gets 50% of profit
Private/'in family'	Must file accounts
	Public domain
	Extra costs with accountants

Mark scheme

Level	Mark	Descriptor
	No mark	Non-rewardable material
Level 1	1–2	A simple statement of one advantage with limited development.
Level 2	3–4	Two advantages are given with some limited development of each.
Level 3	5–6	Two advantages are given, with some well reasoned development to support the points given.

Chapter 20: **The importance of limited liability**

1   What is meant by the term 'sole trader'?

2   What is meant by the term 'limited liability'?

3   What is meant by the term 'unlimited liability'?

4   What is meant by the term 'shareholder'?

5   What is meant by a 'limited company'?

6   Explain how the day-to-day control in a sole trader differs from the control in a limited company.

7   Is unlimited liability likely to be less risky than limited liability for the owner of a business? Explain your answer.

Jane Cowell set up as an interior decorator operating as a sole trader. She invested £20,000 of her own money to get it going. She now owes £50,000 to suppliers.

8   If Jane closed the business how much might she lose? Explain your answer.

9   If Jane had set up as a limited company called JC Ltd how much might she lose? Explain your answer.

10 Explain two reasons why John Rudd, setting up as a fishmonger, might be better off as a sole trader than a limited company.

Suggested answers

1 A sole trader is a business where there is only one owner who makes all the decisions about the business, gets all the profit and is personally responsible for all the debts of the business.

2 Limited liability is where owners (shareholders) are liable (responsible) only for the amount of money he or she has put into the company. They are not personally liable for debts.

3 Unlimited liability is where the business owner is always responsible for the debts of the business. He or she has a legal obligation to settle all debts. There is no limit to their responsibility.

4 A shareholder is someone who has invested in a company and therefore part, owns it. The percentage owned depends on their share ownership. The shareholders are the owners of limited companies.

5 A limited company is a business which is owned by shareholders, who have limited liability.

6 The sole trader has more control over day-to-day operations, e.g. hours worked than in a limited company. The sole trader does not have to file accounts for public scrutiny. The sole trader keeps all the profit whereas a limited company has to split the profits between the shareholders. In a limited company control may be shared between the shareholders who may not all agree on decisions/direction.

7 No. Having limited liability is less risky because the owners only risk losing what they have agreed to put into the business. If the business does badly they can only lose the value of their shares. Unlimited liability is far more risky, as the owners stand to lose the money they have put in and have to pay off debts even if it means they have to sell their personal assets to raise the money.

8 Jane would lose £70,000. This would comprise the £20,000 she invested plus she still owes the £50,000 even though she has closed the business. It is Jane who owes the money not the business.

9 Jane would lose £20,000. This is the money she invested. She would not have to pay the money owed to the suppliers as the business owed that debt, not Jane herself. Her liability is limited to the amount she agreed to put into the business.

10 The fishmonger is likely to be a small business with not much to pay out for machinery or supplies. As such he will not need much external finance, i.e. other investors. He may want to maintain his privacy. So by being a sole trader he will not have to publish accounts. He may want to work flexible hours. As a sole trader he can decide for himself what hours he works. Also, whatever profit he makes, he keeps. Sole traders may find it easier to get trade credit than limited companies because they are liable for debts and so the creditor can expect them to have to sell off personal possessions to pay off debts. There may be some tax advantages to being a sole trader and in addition, the sole trader can take money out of the business whenever they want (assuming there is money there to access).

Chapter 21: **Start-up legal and tax issues**

1.   VAT is a tax on

  A   sales

  B   income

  C   profit

  D   property

  Select **one** answer.

  Answer A

Comments
A Correct – is it about Value Added.
B Incorrect – this would be income tax.
C Incorrect – this would be income tax or corporation tax.
D Incorrect – this would be council tax.

2.   National Insurance contributions are a tax on

  A   sales

  B   income

  C   profit

  D   property

  Select **one** answer.

  Answer B

Comments
A Incorrect – this would be VAT.
B Correct – all workers pay this for state benefits.
C Incorrect – this would be income tax or corporation tax.
D Incorrect – this would be council tax.

3.   A sole trader must keep financial records because

  A   suppliers have a right to see them

  B   customers have a right to see them

  C   they must be available for inspection by HM Revenue & Customs

  D   all sole traders have to pay both Corporation Tax, Employers' National Insurance contributions and VAT

  Select **one** answer.

  Answer C

Comments
A Incorrect – suppliers do not have the right to view a sole trader's financial records.
B Incorrect – it does not concern them.
C Correct – these records are a legal requirement for assessing taxes due.
D Incorrect – sole traders do not pay corporation tax.

Chapter 21: Start-up legal and tax issues

Lara York has worked for three years at a computer repair business. She now wants to set up her own business specialising in computer repairs for other businesses.

She is drawing up a business plan. One issue is what to call her business. 'Lara York Computer Repairs' is one possibility but it is a rather long name. 'York Repairs' would be snappier, but will it give the right impression to her customers?

She has taken some advice about tax matters and has found out that her tax affairs will be different depending on whether she sets up as a sole trader or as a limited company. Whichever she chooses, keeping financial records will be essential. In her first couple of years, her business will probably not have sales of more than £50,000, so she does not think she will need to register with HM Revenue & Customs for VAT. Nor does she intend to employ anyone to start with, so that will cut down the paper work. However, she is not looking forward to keeping records and acting as an unpaid tax collector for the government. Nor is she looking forward to having to calculate how much tax she should pay on her earnings or profits.

1. Explain **two** types of tax that Lara York's business might have to pay. (6)

Indicative content

If sole trader

- **Income tax** = Net earnings/profit
- **National Insurance contributions** – Flat rate, % of profit

If company

- **Corporation tax** – On profit of company
- **National Insurance contributions**

Mark scheme

2 marks for identifying two types of tax that she might pay. Up to 2 marks for explaining these taxes in relation to Lara's business. For example, If Lara set up as a sole trader she would pay income tax. (1 mark) This is a tax on the earnings of employees in a business (1 mark) In the case of a sole trader, who is the sole owner of the business, income tax is paid by the owner on their earnings rather than a tax on any profits of the business, as all profits are taken by the single owner. (1 mark)

2. Analyse why keeping financial records is essential for Lara York once she has set up her business. (4)

Indicative content

- Pay correct VAT
- Pay correct NIC
- Pay correct income tax/corporation tax
- Legal requirement
- Avoid build up of problems, e.g. unpaid tax
- Build relationship with tax office
- True indication of company financial stability
- Keep up to date
- Aware of any problems arising/anticipation

Mark scheme

Up to 4 marks for analysis of the reasons for keeping financial records. For example Keeping financial records is vital for legal reasons, but also to help the business run effectively. (1 mark) Lara requires records of her sales and costs to calculate income tax or corporation tax to be paid to the government. (1 mark) Although she is unlikely to earn enough to pay VAT, HM Revenue & Customs require businesses to keep records and may investigate to check that the correct tax has been paid. (1 mark) Records will also be vital to make sure the business is up-to-date and can anticipate problems that may arise. Records may show, for example, that payments are often late, which could suggest a cash flow problem in future. (1 mark)

3. Lara has come up with the idea of calling the business Royal Kare – based on an anagram of her name. In your opinion would Royal Kare Computers be an appropriate name for this business? Justify your answer.   (6)

Indicative content

Royal Kare Computers

- Founder's name
- Informative
- Memorable
- Links care and PCs
- Sounds upmarket
- Quirky spelling gets interest
- Short
- Not legal if a company, as it would need Ltd on end
- May have problems registering if the word Royal was misleading

Mark scheme

Level	Mark	Descriptor
	No mark	Non-rewardable material
Level 1	1–2	A choice will be made with poorly developed justification and supported by limited examples. For example, 'Yes, it is a name that is easy to remember.'
Level 2	3–4	A choice will be made with some developed justification and supported by some good examples. For example, 'Yes. It is a name that is easy to remember and could attract interest due to its quirky spelling. It also includes the business that Lara is running. The Royal may indicate an up-market product and a good service.'
Level 3	5–6	A choice will be made with a clearly developed justification and supported by excellent examples. For example, 'The name would need to include Ltd at the end if the business was a limited company. However, the name itself has a number of advantages. It is easy to remember, indicates the nature of the business and has a quirky spelling which could make it stand out from other businesses. The name Royal also implies an up-market product, which could imply a good service. Care would need to be taken that this name could be registered.'

Chapter 21: **Start-up legal and tax issues**

1 What is meant by the term 'VAT'?

2 What is 'income tax'?

3 What is 'corporation tax'?

4 Explain how National Insurance contributions work.

5 What is the role of HM Revenue and Customs?

6 State two reasons why it is important for businesses to keep records for tax purposes.

7 State two reasons why it is wise for businesses to keep records of their customers.

Romano Tilson trained as a shoemaker and repairer. He had a dream of opening his own business. He was considering calling his business 'Cobblers' as this reflected what he did.

8 Why might his friend have advised him to call his business 'Sole Mate' rather than 'Cobblers'?

9 As a shoe repairer, what sort of legal responsibilities might Romano have in running his business?

10 Give two benefits of having a unique trading name to Romano.

Suggested answers

1 VAT is Value Added Tax, a tax paid by businesses to HMR&C but passed on to consumers as higher prices. It is a tax paid on the value added by the business.

2 Income tax is a tax paid by workers on part of their wages or salaries. Sole traders pay this as well. Limited companies do not pay this.

3 Corporation tax is a tax paid by companies on their profits. Sole traders and workers do not pay this.

4 National Insurance contributions are a tax paid on the earnings of workers, but payment is split between the worker and the employer. The employer deducts the tax from the wages before the worker gets their pay packet and sends both contributions (theirs and the workers) to the government.

5 The role of HM Revenue and Customs is to collect all the taxes due to the government. These include VAT, NICs, income tax and corporation tax.

6 Records need to be kept in case an inspection is made. The records are available to the tax authorities. Records must be kept so that businesses pay tax on a regular basis. If they don't they may face a massive bill for tax. Records must also be kept to ensure a business doesn't pay too much tax as that would hinder its cash flow.

7 Businesses keep records so that if the customer contacts them with a query they can see the history of the transaction. The business can also use the records to contact the customer with any special offers. This is a good way of getting repeat business as well as understanding customer needs more effectively.

8 Romano's friend advised him that a memorable name was important and needed to give customers a hint of what the business was about. Both names did that but Sole Mate had a better 'ring' to it and was a bit of a clever play with words whilst 'Cobblers' may have sounded funny rather than the name of a proper business. The word 'cobblers' is also used in slang as a derogatory term so might have put some customers off.

9 Given that Romano will have to use machinery, he will have to abide by health and safety laws. He will have to meet consumer laws such as the Sale of Goods Act and the Trade Descriptions Act and also to ensure that he has the appropriate licenses and insurance to allow him to operate his business.

10 Possible benefits include the fact that people may remember the name more easily, may be able to find his business in Yellow Pages or other directories and search engines, may be able to associate what his business is with the name and may provide a way of differentiating his business from those of his rivals.

Chapter 22: **Customer satisfaction**

1. Which **two** of the following are the best examples of effective customer service?

    Select **two** answers.

    A   Selling large quantities to customers

    B   Fulfilling customer orders accurately

    C   Holding a Christmas sale to dispose of stock

    D   Dealing promptly with customer complaints

    E   Having no repeat purchases

    Answer B and D

Comments
A Incorrect – selling large quantities does not necessarily mean high levels of customer service.
B Correct – customers have a right to expect to get what they ordered and this will improve the experience they have with the business.
C Incorrect – this is not a service just a means of raising revenue. Having a sale does not necessarily mean customers will also get good service.
D Correct – this reduces customer distress and makes them feel wanted thus improving their experience of the business.
E Incorrect – this is possibly the result of poor customer service.

2. Hay's is a small pizza business offering either take-away pizza from its shop or a pizza delivery service.

    Select **one** answer.

    A   otherwise stocks would be too low

    B   it creates more jobs

    C   it helps improve cash flow

    D   it leads to customer satisfaction

    Answer D

Comments
A Incorrect – it is not relevant.
B Incorrect – delivery is about the customer not employees.
C Incorrect – the opposite would happen.
D Correct – it fulfils a customer need and should lead to repeat purchases.

3. Witton Industrial Ceramics is a business that manufactures and sells pottery. Repeat purchases from customers are **most likely** to be important to the success of Witton Industrial Ceramics because they increase

    A   fixed costs

    B   prices

    C   sales turnover

    D   venture capital

Select **one** answer.

Answer C

Comments
A Incorrect – they might increase variable costs.
B Incorrect – repeat purchases do not necessarily lead to an increase in prices.
C Correct – more sales means more money passing from the customer to the business.
D Incorrect – this is something that is put into a business to help get it started.

Chapter 22: **Customer satisfaction**

Libby Headon trained as a plumber ten years ago and set up her own plumbing business. Although some of her work is for building companies, most of her time is spent dealing with household repairs.

Libby's business has three unique selling points. First, the quality of her work is excellent. Second, her charges are very reasonable. Third, she is a woman. Many female customers say they prefer having a woman doing repairs in their house. They feel safer and they trust the quality of the work.

Libby has a tried and tested formula when someone rings her up. She arranges when she can do the work and tells the customer what she charges for a call out and the rate per hour of work. If on the day of the appointment she is running late, she always lets her clients know by telephoning them. Once at the customer's house, she gives a quote for the work. Once the work is completed, she gives the customer three of her business cards. One is for them to keep in case they need to contact her. The other two she asks her customers to give to friends or relations in case they should ever need a plumber. If there is ever any problem with the work she has done, she calls back as quickly as possible to fix it.

Many plumbers pay to advertise in publications like *Yellow Pages*. Libby Headon has not spent any money on advertising for the past eight years. All her work comes from previous customers or through word of mouth recommendations.

1. Explain the importance of (a) quality of work and (b) dealing with complaints to the success of Libby Headon's business. (6)

Indicative content

(a)

- Customer satisfaction
- reduces the need to return to fix problems which adds to costs
- builds trust and generates customer loyalty
- Repeat business
- Recommendations reduce the cost of advertising and help generate business
- No hidden charges

(b)

- Trust
- Loyalty
- Happy to recommend
- Free adverts

Mark scheme

Up to 3 marks for each, in relation to Libby Headon's business. For example, 'Quality of work is important for a plumbing business. Flooding, problems with sewage and faulty water appliances, for example, all need to be repaired effectively or they can lead to major problems. (1 mark) If Libby's work is of good quality, then it helps to build loyal customers for her service. (1 mark) Customers who are pleased with the quality of work are likely to be repeat customers of the business. They are also likely to recommend it to others, both of which could increase profits.' (1 mark)

2. How does repeat business contribute to the success of Libby's business? (3)

Indicative content

- No need to advertise
- Trust from women customers
- Always has work
- Improved cash flow
- Builds customer base and increases sales
- Increases revenue and profit

Mark scheme

Up to 3 marks for explanation of how repeat business contributes to the success of Libby's business. For example, 'Repeat business for Libby means that the same customers are using her services over and over again. They are likely to be women, who feel safe and prefer other women doing work in their house. (1 mark) Repeat business can make sure that there is a constant revenue and cash flow coming in to the business, which can reduce risk. (1 mark) It may also save on promotional methods such as advertising if the same customers are using the business over and over again and possibly passing this information to others.' (1 mark)

3. 'A successful plumbing business is all about customer service'. Do you agree with this statement? Justify your answer. (6)

Indicative content

No

- Customer service is never 'free' – it may increase costs. Price may be more important than good service to some people.
- How often is a plumber needed? Is it a one-off service to customers or is there repeat business?
- Other factors in the business may be as important, such as controlling cash flow.

Yes

- Good customer service means customers are more likely to use her again – this generates additional business.
- Good customer service may mean value for money.
- Good customer service increases customer loyalty and increases the likelihood of repeat purchase.
- Less 'selling' involved which can be time consuming and increases costs.
- Word of mouth selling/recommendations – a much cheaper way of advertising the business to generate more sales.
- Information to customers – known price – improves customer confidence and trust.
- Complaints sorted immediately – customers feel confident in using her service and then come back again – increases likelihood of future sales.

Mark scheme

Level	Mark	Descriptor
	No mark	Non-rewardable material
Level 1	1–2	A choice will be made with poorly developed justification and supported by limited examples. For example, 'Yes, because good service brings in customers.'
Level 2	3–4	A choice will be made with some developed justification and supported by some good examples. At the bottom end of the range the answer will be unbalanced with one side only given any attention. For example, 'Yes. Good services ensure that customers will return to use the services of a business. Loyal customers not only bring repeat business but give recommendations. Poor customer service can damage reputation.' At the top end of the range there will be some balance given.
Level 3	5–6	A choice will be made with a clearly developed justification and supported by excellent examples. There will be balance to the answer and a conclusion will be given. For example, 'On the one hand good customer service may not be absolutely essential. For example, in the case of a plumber, the service may not be needed that often and many single jobs are done for different people. Also, providing good service may come at the cost of higher prices and customers may look for cheaper alternatives. However, poor service is likely to damage the reputation of a business. Word of mouth may spread information that a poor service is provided and this may reduce the number of people asking for work to be done. In plumbing, which is a technical service, this could be vital. So overall, a successful plumbing business is all about customer service.'

Chapter 22: **Customer satisfaction**

1   What is meant by the term 'customer service'?

2   What is meant by the term 'customer satisfaction'?

3   What is meant by the term 'repeat purchase?

4   What is meant by the term 'customer loyalty'?

5   Why is 'word of mouth' advertising of value to a business?

6   A theatre operates a discount scheme for customers who attend regularly. How does this benefit the theatre and the customer?

7   Theresa Green Garden Centres has set up a website. State two ways in which this might improve customer satisfaction.

How might the following use customer service to gain a competitive advantage?

8   A village grocer compared with a national supermarket.

9   A furniture company offering same day delivery compared with one that books deliveries weeks ahead.

10 A clothes shop which offers a 'no quibble' refund policy compared with one that offers only a credit note.

Suggested answers

1 Customer service is the experience a customer has when dealing with a business and the extent to which the experience meets or exceeds customer needs and expectations.

2 Customer satisfaction is a measure of how the good or the service given meets the expectations of the customer.

3 Repeat purchase is where customers return to the same shop or for the same product (or both) on a regular basis because they are happy with what they have got. All businesses would generally want this.

4 Customer loyalty is where the product offered by a business has made such an impact on the customer that s/he keeps buying it because it satisfies a need. Price and substitutes do not feature highly when the customer comes to purchase the item.

5 The value is that it is a good way to promote a product. If one customer tells another about their experience it is accepted better than any promotion by the company. This is because the first user is not trying to sell anything. Their evidence is considered more genuine and first hand. Buyers query products less if they are recommended to buy it by someone else.

6 The theatre gains by having more customers so its revenue will go up and probably its profits, too. Cash flow is improved. It gets a good reputation. The customer gains by paying less each time they use the theatre so they get better value for money and good customer service.

7 Customers will be able to see what the garden centre has on offer before making a trip to buy. They can see any special deals. They may be able to order online which would be more cost-effective. They may be able to track the progress of their order.

8 The village shop is more convenient for the customer. It may offer a delivery service locally free of charge. It may get special items in for a customer. It may offer a form of trade credit for some customers and can offer a more personal service.

9 Customers tend to prefer to get access to their purchases straight away, so this would be one way of meeting a 'must have' need compared to the other business which delivered at a later date.

10 Customers feel more confident about a purchase if they know they can return it if it is the wrong size, colour etc and get their money back. They are more likely to pay a bit more for that service and are more likely to keep buying from that business. So the business will get a better reputation and customer base.

Chapter 23: Recruiting, training and motivating staff

1. Spitzer's is a small business that has just sent out a job description to applicants for a job. A job description is a document that

   A   shows a candidate's personal details and qualifications

   B   gives a description of the business and what it does

   C   asks a candidate about their name, address and work experience

   D   lists what the applicant would be expected to do if appointed to the job

   Select **one** answer.

   Answer D

Comments
A Incorrect – that is referring to a CV.
B Incorrect – that is background knowledge of the business not the job being advertised.
C Incorrect – this information would appear on a job application form or a CV.
D Correct – it explains the actual tasks of the job being advertised by Spitzer's.

2. Spitzer's is a small business. It has asked applicants for a job to send in a letter of application together with a

   A   curriculum vitae

   B   person specification

   C   job description

   D   set of fringe benefits

   Select **one** answer.

   Answer A

Comments
A Correct – this would tell Spitzer's about the candidate's employment history.
B Incorrect – they would send that to the applicant.
C Incorrect – that would go out with the job advert when seeking applicants.
D Incorrect – these are what the company might offer.

Test yourself answers
Topic 1.4: Making the start-up effective
BUSINESS

3. Which **one** of the following would **always** be illegal under UK law for a small business?

    Select **one** answer.

    A   Making a worker redundant

    B   Paying a female worker less than a male worker for doing exactly the same job

    C   Hiring a younger worker over an older worker who had also applied for the job

    D   Expecting workers to work in very hot conditions

    Answer B

    The key to the answer to this question is the emboldened word 'always'. There is legislation regarding age and working conditions, for example, but the options offered may be possible under the right circumstances.

Comments
A Incorrect – a business can do this if the job does not exist any more or is not needed.
B Correct – this is discrimination on the grounds of gender and this is illegal.
C Incorrect – the younger worker might be more suitable for the job.
D Incorrect – this is not something which can be legislated against and may be part of the contract of employment.

Chapter 23: **Recruiting, training and motivating staff**

Feeman's is a small business that specialises in converting cars to make them suitable for disabled users. The job is highly skilled. It involves taking a standard car and fixing lifts and hoists for wheelchairs, converting gear boxes and altering control panels.

It currently has a vacancy for a mechanic. The successful applicant would need to have extensive experience of car repairs and bodywork. They would have to show that they had a positive attitude, were well motivated and could work in a team.

Two people applied for the job. The older male applicant, aged 56, met all the requirements of the job description and the person specification, had better experience and qualifications than the younger, female applicant aged 25. He also had a more positive attitude. The owner of Feeman's decided, though, to appoint the 25 year old. The older person would soon have to retire and the owner thought that the female applicant would 'add glamour to the workshop'. There were too many older workers at Feeman's anyway.

1. Describe the likely process of recruiting a new mechanic at Feeman's from advertising for the job to offering the job to the successful applicant. (3)

Indicative content

- Job advert
- Application forms
- Job particulars and job description
- Person specification.
- Interview
- Competency testing
- References
- Offer

Mark scheme

Up to 3 marks for description of the stages in the recruitment and selection process. For example, Feeman's would first advertise the vacancy. It would send out application forms, job particulars, giving information and the business, and a job description, giving information about the job, to applicants. (1 mark) It would also draw up a person specification which would identify the type of person they thought would be suitable, stating some of the characteristics they would need to be successful. (1 mark) Applicants would be shortlisted and then interviewed. A suitable candidate will then be chosen who meets most of the criteria set out in the job description and person specification. (1 mark)

2. The older applicant 'had a more positive attitude'. Explain, using examples, what this means.(3)

Indicative content

* More favourable, constructive opinions.

Examples

- Looked for answers
- Asked questions
- Smiled
- Interested in company not just wages
- Prepared to work flexibly to fit in with needs of business
- Willing to go the 'extra mile'
- Proactive – was able to give advice and offer suggestions
- Talked with other staff
- Keen to be involved
- Supportive

Mark scheme

Up to 3 marks for explaining the statement. For example, 'A more positive attitude means that someone, in this case the older applicant, has views that were more constructive, 'better' and favourable than the other applicant for the job. (1 mark) Examples of this could have been that he was interested in the company and the job and not just the wages, (1 mark) that he made suggestions on how he could do his job better or that he appeared to be willing to work extremely hard and do whatever it takes, within reason, to get the job done effectively. (1 mark)

3. Do you think that Feeman's has broken the law in appointing the younger applicant? Justify your answer. (6)

Indicative content

The passage suggests that the owner did not make a decision based on the criteria of the job description or the person specification. The older worker fulfilled all the criteria but the owner appears to have appointed the younger female worker for other reasons that would be considered unfair and illegal. The older worker would appear to have a strong case to argue that he had been discriminated against on the grounds of age. Businesses have to keep copies of the documentation they collect when appointing a worker and the worker has the right to see this documentation. The older worker could ask for this information in arguing his case.

Mark scheme

Level	Mark	Descriptor
	No mark	Non-rewardable material
Level 1	1–2	A choice will be made with poorly developed justification and supported by limited examples. For example, 'Yes. The owner did not want more older workers.'
Level 2	3–4	A choice will be made with some developed justification and supported by some good examples. For example, 'Yes. The older applicant appears to have more experience and a more positive attitude. But the younger applicant was appointed because the business did not want more older workers. This is breaking the Age Discrimination Act.'
Level 3	5–6	A choice will be made with a clearly developed justification and supported by excellent examples. For example, 'Yes. There may have been some reasons for appointing the younger candidate and the application did allow females and people of all ages to apply. But the older candidate seemed to have better experience and meet more of the criteria that the business was looking for. It appears that the final judgment has been based on the owner not wanting to appoint older people and reasons that were not part of the criteria – 'glamour in the workshop'. This is against the Age Discrimination Act, which prevents discrimination on grounds of age in appointment and selection. If proven, Feeman's would have been breaking the law.'

Chapter 23: **Recruiting, training and motivating staff**

1   What is meant by the term 'job description'?

2   What is meant by the term 'person specification'?

3   What is meant by the term 'curriculum vitae?

4   State two reasons why it is important for businesses to conduct interviews of applicants.

5   What is meant by the term 'on-the-job training'?

6   What is meant by the term 'off-the-job training'?

7   State four ways a business could try to motivate its staff.

8   'Bridget has a really positive attitude.' Explain why this might be important to a business.

9   State four ways that a business cannot use to discriminate against applicants or its workforce.

10   Explain the steps a business might take to recruit and select a web designer.

Suggested answers

1   A job description is a document that describes the duties of a worker and their status in an organisation.

2   A person specification is a profile of the type of person needed for a job including their skills and qualities.

3   A curriculum vitae or CV is a document where a person can identify their strengths, experience and qualifications as well as giving basic details such as their name and address.

4   They would do this because the person might have written things on an application form or CV that are not true. Verbal questions at an interview can reveal this. Also, the business would get a 'feel' for the person and may be better able to decide if they would fit in with the rest of the staff. Interviews are a two-way process, so it is also useful to give the candidate a chance to see if they would like to work for the business.

5   On-the-job training is where a person learns about the job in the workplace itself, whilst doing that job, usually working alongside someone more experienced, for example, a checkout operator learning how to operate a till in a shop.

6   Off-the-job training is where a person is sent to a specialist training provider for dedicated skills training, usually away from the place where they work.

7   Examples could include higher wages, good working conditions, sports club membership, private health care, company newsletters, meetings, flexitime, empowerment and respect.

8   This is important because Bridget's attitude will rub off on other people and they will think positively rather than negatively meaning she is more likely to look for solutions rather than dwelling on problems. The atmosphere at work will be better. More work will get done. Bridget will come across well to customers and this will show the company in a good light. Bridget will look at what can be done, not what cannot be done. It will make her a good team player so all round the business will get better.

9   A business cannot discriminate on grounds of age, gender, race, culture, disability and religion.

10 The business would draw up a job description and then a person specification. It would advertise in a suitable place, either a trade magazine or on the Internet, as these could be where web designers might look. It would design an application form and information for applicants. When it received applications it would consider application forms and short list applicants. It would then carry out interviews. As part of the interview the business would want the applicant to show they could actually design a website, so it could include practical aspects as well as verbal questions. After the interview the business would select a person for the job and then offer the successful applicant the job. If the applicant accepts then an official letter is sent confirming the job offer.

Practice exam questions

Sharon Kocabas was environmentally friendly. She sorted all her rubbish into different bags for recycling. It was time-consuming and Sharon wished it would happen automatically. Then the idea hit her to design a bin where you put the rubbish in the top, it read the bar code and sorted the rubbish into appropriate coloured bags via a rotating carousel. Refuse collectors simply picked up the bags and put them onto the wagons. Sharon realised this had potential with a USP, but needed to be marketed properly. She decided to call it BINSKA in order to get the idea across that it was a bin and it scanned. SCANBIN didn't sound right and using the K added a bit of class, she thought.

In creating her marketing mix Sharon focused on promotion to show how it worked. She felt the product spoke for itself, price would not be an issue at £149.99 and she would sell it through DIY outlets and to local councils. BINSKA would also supply the bags, which are recyclable, and took out a patent on them. Sharon got support from the bank, but it advised her to make BINSKA a private limited company to protect any investment. Sharon could not do it all by herself. She needed someone to look after the record-keeping such as VAT, National Insurance, tax and wages. She needed sales staff to sell the product, but who also had detailed knowledge of the product to ensure customers were happy and would recommend her product to others. General office staff were needed to assist with the day-to-day running of the business. Sharon advertised for staff using a variety of adverts appropriate for the job. In order to keep staff motivated and to make them feel valued, Sharon introduced pay incentives and free health care.

(a) Which **two** of the following **best** describe Sharon's reason for offering free health care? She wants to?

   A   motivate the staff to work hard for her

   B   improve her record keeping

   C   meet customer needs

   D   promote the image of the product

   E   advertise for new staff

   F   keep staff from leaving

Answer A and F

Examiner's comment
A Correct – they are getting something, which makes them feel valued.
B Incorrect – it's not relevant to motivating her staff.
C Incorrect – her offer is about staff not customers.
D Incorrect – the image is for the customers not the staff.
E Incorrect – she can advertise anyway whether she offers this or not.
F Correct – it is a reward that staff might not receive at another business.

(b) Explain how Sharon plans to deliver good customer service. (3)

Indicative content

- Specialist sales staff, not one-size-fits-all staff
- Distribution via suitable outlets/on-site advice
- Convenience as DIY outlets are nationwide/councils similar
- Aware of value of word of mouth advertising
- Repeat purchases
- Selling to councils so householders can get benefits without initial outlay
- Large orders could generate discounts

Mark scheme

Explain that customer service refers to the experience the customer has in dealing with a business. (1 mark) Sharon employed specialist sales staff with knowledge of the product to make sure customers understood the product and to make sure that their needs were catered for when buying the bin. (1 mark) This was likely to lead to good customer service – customers will have a positive experience and may recommend the product to others. (1 mark)

(c) Evaluate Sharon's marketing mix for launching BINSKA. (6)

Indicative content

- Unique product/USP
- New product
- Promotion
- 'Live' promotion
- Place identified
- Price appropriate for product and market
- Recover initial costs quickly
- Consistency of mix, e.g. high price, all aspects have a 'quality' feel
- Appropriate promotion/not flyers
- Has kept offline/keeps control
- Memorable/appropriate trading name

Mark scheme

Level	Mark	Descriptor
	No mark	Non-rewardable material
Level 1	1–2	A simple description of the elements of the marketing mix with examples from the Case Study. For example, 'The mix is the 4Ps, price, product, promotion and place. She is charging £149.99 for the bin'. Or 'it would work because it has a catchy name and so it says what it is.'
Level 2	3–4	The elements would be better described and each would be exemplified, with some attempt at evaluative comments. For example, 'the product is very clear as it is the bin, the price is £149.99, she is focusing on promotion which is a good idea to show how it works, and the place is via DIY outlets.' Or 'using DIY outlets and the council is a good way to get the product to the customers.'
Level 3	5–6	The evaluation would be more considered with pros and cons identified, e.g. 'the price is right but will the council be the right customer?' There will be sequential comments. For example, 'The mix is set right because it is a quality product, backed up with a quality promotion and readily available to the target market.' Or 'the marketing mix is adventurous, but maybe the price is too high for something which is not tried and tested'.
Level 4	7–8	The evaluation would take into account all the elements and whether as a 'mix' it works. There will be linked reasons leading to each other and the final outcome as to whether it would bring success. A conclusion will be drawn and justified. There could be comments of how the mix could be adapted with improvements suggested. For example 'The marketing mix is adventurous. Perhaps the price is too high for a new product onto the market which is not tried and tested and has not yet developed a brand image and a loyal customer base. So charging a price of less than £100, for example, might be more advisable initially.'

Case study

Norford's is a small business that manufactures testing equipment. Its customers are other businesses that need to test the quality of their own products. For example, a crane manufacturing company might want to test the strength of a piece of steel when put under pressure. At what stress level will it snap? An aircraft manufacturer might want to test at what temperature – both high and low – a component might explode due to extreme heat or cold.

Norford's operates in a market with only a small number of competitors. Like many businesses, it can set its own prices. However, this is very different from some of the firms from which it buys. Some of these suppliers have to accept the price that the market dictates. One example is suppliers who manufacture steel. Steel firms produce a commodity product. The price of steel is determined on international markets like the London Metal Exchange. Here buyers and sellers of steel from all over the world meet to agree trades, which set the price for steel. When demand for steel falls, even by a few per cent, there can be a large fall in the price of steel. Norford's uses a lot of steel in its products. Changes in steel prices can have a major effect on Norford's costs – either increasing them or cutting them.

Interest rates are another major cost that Norford's has to face. It has loans and an overdraft of £50,000. If interest rates fall, this can help cut the interest payments that the business has to make. If interest rates rise, the increase in costs can be damaging to the cash flow of the business.

Interest rates are likely to fall if the economy suffers a downturn. When this happens orders for equipment from Norford's can fall dramatically, as the customers it supplies cut back on their spending. The situation only gets better when consumer spending picks up again. Until that time firms will not feel confident about ordering new equipment; why should they if they do not think they will sell what they are producing?

One positive aspect of a downturn in the economy for Norford's is that the value of the pound is likely to fall. This makes its exports more price competitive. Without a fall in the exchange rate, the drop in orders could be even greater.

In a time of economic downturn, Norford's has some difficult decisions to make. It employs 11 workers. Should it make some workers redundant? If the firm is making a loss, the two owners of the business will not be able to take any profit out of the business. If this happens then Norford's has to investigate other ways in which it could cut costs. Could it squeeze its suppliers more by negotiating lower prices? Could it use the fall in the exchange rate to put up its prices to foreign customers?

Suggested discussion points/answers

1. How might Norford's be affected by each of the following?

(a) There is a sharp cut in worldwide demand for oil.

(b) The Bank of England decides to raise interest rates.

(c) The value of the pound rises against the euro.

(d) The economy goes into recession.

(a)
- depends on how much oil it uses in production
- If it is a major factor used in production then costs could rise significantly

(b)
- Costs increase – the interest it pays on loans will rise
- Demand falls as consumers' disposable income falls
- Will have an adverse effect on cash flow
- Interest on any savings increases

(c)
- exports become less competitive
- Possible fall in demand from overseas
- More competitive in the UK against foreign imports
- The price it pays for any imported materials will fall – they have to give up fewer pounds to get the same amount of foreign currency.

(d)

- Demand falls

- Lay off staff

- May have to close

- Norford's owners could lose their investment if the business does have to close

2. Who are the stakeholders in Norford's highlighted in the passage?

- Suppliers

- Customers

- Workers

- Owners

3. How might an increase in demand for testing equipment affect Norford's stakeholders?

- Suppliers = positive, more supplies needed

- Customers = positive, able/willing to buy more, more confident

  = negative, may have to wait longer for goods

- Workers = positive, more jobs, wage increases, greater job security

- Owners = positive, profit, expanding business

Chapter 24: Demand and supply

1. The price of oil rises on world markets. This is most likely to be because

    A the demand for oil has fallen

    B the supply of oil has risen

    C the supply of oil has risen faster than the demand for oil

    D the demand for oil has risen faster than the supply of oil

    Select **one** answer.

    Answer D

Comments
A Incorrect – this might cause prices to fall.
B Incorrect – because a rise in the supply of oil will mean more is available for sale and if demand stays the same then prices will fall – there will be a surplus.
C Incorrect – this would cause prices to fall – for the same reason as in B – a surplus.
D Correct – more buyers are competing for fewer products so they will be prepared to pay more and this tends to force prices up.

2. Jake Wooley runs a flower shop in London. He buys most of his flowers from a supplier in the Netherlands. The supplier in the Netherlands increases its prices. Jake's decision about whether he puts up the price of flowers to his customers because of this cost increase is most likely to depend on

    A how much insurance he pays

    B how big the increase is in the cost of the flowers he buys

    C the amount of flowers he sells each week

    D which supplier he buys his flowers from

    E how large a proportion of his total costs is made up from buying flowers

    Select **two** answers.

    Answer B and E

Comments
A Incorrect – the cost of insurance has not changed. If this fixed cost stays the same, there is no reason for Jake to put up his prices.
B Correct – if the increase in cost is very small, like 1 per cent, Jake is unlikely to put his prices. If he puts up his prices, he could lose customers. A 1 per cent increase in price is probably not worth the risk of this happening. However, if the cost of flowers to Jake is very large, then he would have no option but to increase his own prices. Flowers are likely to be a very important cost for Jake. Say the cost of flowers to Jake doubled. A doubling in cost will have a large impact on his total costs. Without an increase in prices, he would probably start to make a loss.
C Incorrect – the amount of flowers he sells each week is unlikely to affect whether or not he puts up his prices. A large seller of flowers will be just as affected in percentage terms as a small seller of flowers by a price increase. For example, if Tesco, a huge seller of flowers, experiences a 10 per cent increase in its costs of flowers, it faces exactly the same problems as Jake who only sells a tiny fraction of the number of flowers sold by Tesco. They both have to decide how to react to the 10 per cent increase.
D Incorrect – the question asks about what Jake's reaction would be to an increase in the cost of flowers. Whether he buys from a Dutch supplier or, for example, a UK supplier, he faces exactly the same problem of the increase in costs.
E Correct – the larger the proportion of total cost made up from flowers, the more likely Jake is to increase his own prices. If the cost of flowers were just 1 per cent of his costs, an increase in the price he has to pay for the flowers will have hardly any impact on his own costs. Hence, he is unlikely to increase his own prices. However, if the cost of flowers were half of his total costs, then even fairly small increases in the cost of flowers will have a significant impact on his total costs. The bigger the proportion of his cost made up from flowers, the more likely he is to raise his prices after an increase in his own cost of buying flowers.

3. Dylan Parkes has re-opened a former tin mine in Cornwall. He produces a small amount of tin which he sells at auction in London. He also uses the mine as a tourist attraction, charging visitors to come and see old workings. Which **one** of the following is **most likely** to be true about his business?

Select **one** answer.

A   He has to accept whatever price is set at auction for his tin

B   He has no control over the price he sets for visitors to see the mine

C   He cannot charge a higher ticket price to visitors in July and August than at other times of the year

D   He can decide for what price he sells his tin

Answer A

Comments
A Correct – it is a commodity so he is a price taker.
B Incorrect – he owns the business and can decide on the price to charge for visitors. This is not a commodity so he can be a price maker.
C Incorrect – visitors to Cornwall tend to be higher in the summer months and as demand is likely to be higher he could charge higher prices.
D Incorrect – as it is a commodity the price is set on international markets.

Over to you answers
Topic 1.5: The economic context
BUSINESS

Chapter 24: Demand and supply

Gillam's is a small firm that makes steel parts for machines. Over the past twelve months it has seen the price of steel double. Steel is a commodity that is traded on world markets. In recent years, the demand for steel from China and other fast growing economies has increased rapidly. The size of the Chinese economy is doubling every seven years. China's cities are seeing a construction boom and steel is in very heavy demand for new buildings.

Gillam's has no choice but to pay the higher prices for steel. However, it is being hard hit by the price increases. Its customers are putting pressure on the company not to put up its prices. They are hinting that they will buy their parts from a different supplier if Gillam's chooses to go ahead with a price rise. On the other hand, Gillam's has worked closely with many of its customers for a number of years giving excellent service. Competitors have also been putting up their prices. So Gillam's has made the decision to raise its prices too by 10 per cent. Otherwise, it faced making a loss and it could in the long term have been forced to close.

1. Steel is a commodity. Its price is determined in international markets. Explain why the price of steel might rise on these markets. (3)

Indicative content

- Demand
- Supply
- Price where D=S
- Where customers and suppliers agree on same price

Mark scheme

Up to 3 marks for explanation. The key to the marks is for showing the process through which the price may rise. For example, 'Firms who use steel in production will want to buy it and this represents the demand for steel. Steel manufacturers will offer steel for sale and this represents the supply of steel. (1 mark) The interaction between the buyers of steel and the sellers of steel will determine the price, which is agreed on international markets. (1 mark) If the demand for steel rises and supply is constant then this causes a shortage of steel on the markets and this causes the price to rise.' (1 mark)

2. Analyse **two** possible effects on Gillam's if it had not increased its prices by 10 per cent. (6)

Indicative content

- May buy less steel
- Lose orders, revenue and reduced profit
- Increase total costs and lose profit
- Depends what rivals did
- Depends on whether its sales would have risen and by how much
- Depends on the size of their costs in relation to their revenue
- Cash flow might have been affected – higher expenditure but similar revenue
- Job losses to cut costs
- May have to consider alternatives

Mark scheme

1 mark for each effect identified. Up to 2 marks for further analysis offered. For example, the price of steel had doubled over the past 12 months. If Gillam's had not increased its price by 10% it may not have been able to afford this. (1 mark) As a result it may have had to buy less steel, as it could not afford to pay the higher pieces. (1 mark) If it had less steel then it may not have been able to make as many parts for its customers. (1 mark)

3. Evaluate how Gillam's customers might react to the 10 per cent increase in price. (6)

Indicative content

- Go elsewhere
- Loyalty
- Known product quality
- Customer service
- Pass on price increase
- Absorb cost increase
- Competitors also putting up prices

Mark scheme

Level	Mark	Descriptor
	No mark	Non-rewardable material
Level 1	1–2	A choice will be made with poorly developed justification and supported by limited examples. For example, 'Customers would not pay the higher price and Gillam's would lose customers.'
Level 2	3–4	A choice will be made with some developed justification and supported by some good examples. For example, 'Some machine producers have threatened to move custom elsewhere if the business puts up its price. But not all customers may move elsewhere because other suppliers are having to put their prices up as well. It will depend how far they put their prices up.'
Level 3	5–6	A choice will be made with a clearly developed justification and supported by excellent examples. For example: 'Some machine producers will try to find alternative suppliers and Gillam's may lose customers. But other steel parts manufacturers have also put up their prices. So customers may find that even with a 10% price increase, Gillam's prices are still competitive and remain with the business. Further, Gillam's has an excellent record over the years of providing good service. Changing supplier can be difficult and some businesses customers may prefer to remain with Gillam's.'

4. Discuss whether Gillam's workers have benefited from the 10 per cent price increase. (6)

Indicative content

Yes

- Keep jobs if demand does not fall too much
- Higher price may be able to afford higher wages

No

- Depends on responsiveness of demand to price
- No cash benefit if price rise only covers increase of raw material price rise
- Lose jobs if demand falls

Mark scheme

Level	Mark	Descriptor
	No mark	Non-rewardable material
Level 1	1–2	A choice will be made with poorly developed justification and supported by limited examples. For example, 'Yes. They would have lost their jobs without it.'
Level 2	3–4	A choice will be made with some developed justification and supported by some good examples. For example, 'Yes. The price rise was needed to pay the higher costs of steel. Without this the business would not have been able to afford steel for parts and may have not been able to supply customers. As a result it may have gone out of business.'
Level 3	5–6	A choice will be made with a clearly developed justification and supported by excellent examples. For example, 'Some workers may have lost their jobs in the price rise resulting in customers moving their custom to other producers of parts. However, overall most workers would have kept their jobs. Without the price increase Gillam's may not have been able to pay the higher costs. It could have gone out of business and all workers would have been made redundant.'

Chapter 24: **Demand and supply**

1   What is meant by the term 'demand'?

2   What is meant by the term 'supply'?

3   What is a 'commodity'?

4   What is meant by the term 'price takers'?

5   What is meant by the term 'price makers'?

6   How does a goods market differ from a commodity market?

7   State two reasons why demand for a product might fall.

Eva Grady sells rolls with fillings such as meat for 99p to employees of businesses in a city centre.

8   Explain one way in which a fall in the cost of meat could affect Eva's business.

9   Explain two reasons why Eva might absorb a small rise in the cost of meat rather than pass this on.

10 What could be the effect on Eva's business if she continues to absorb all rises in raw material costs?

Suggested answers

1   Demand is the amount that consumers are willing and able to buy at a given price.

2   Supply is the amount that sellers are willing and able to offer at a given price.

3   A commodity is a raw material which goes into the making of a product.

4   Price takers are businesses that are not able to control the price they get for their products. They must accept the price set by the market. Price takers are often found in commodity markets.

5   Price makers are businesses that have some limited ability to set their own prices.

6   A goods market is for normal everyday products, such as DVDs, clothes, food and petrol. Commodity markets are markets where raw materials used in production such as wheat, sugar, oil, copper, tin etc. are traded.

7   Reasons why the demand for a product might fall include a change in the structure or size of the population, a fall in advertising spending, changes in fashion or tastes, a fall in the price of substitutes, greater competition (better products available elsewhere) and a fall in income.

8   A fall in the cost of meat could benefit Eva as it would be cheaper to make the rolls. So the costs of producing the product would fall. Eva could pass this benefit on in the hope of getting more custom or she could leave prices as they are and make a greater profit on each roll sold.

9   Eva might absorb a rise in the cost of meat rather than pass this on because she may think it is temporary and that the reduction in products will soon right itself. Also, it may push the price over 99p and buyers may be quite sensitive about it going over £1 and so look elsewhere. Eva might also be making enough profit not to notice the loss very much. It might be better to lose a bit of profit rather than pay to change all her adverts.

10 Eva could go out of business if she doesn't make enough money to cover her costs. She could start to use cheaper raw materials or supply smaller portions. This might lead to a loss of business as customers would see a fall in quality so they would go elsewhere.

Chapter 25: **The impact of interest rates**

1. A small bookshop has run an overdraft of £1,000 for the past twelve months. The rate of interest on the overdraft was 8 per cent. The bank has now written to the business saying that its overdraft rate will change to 10 per cent. What will be the increase in its overdraft interest if it borrows £1,000 for another twelve months?

   Select **one** answer.

   A   £100

   B   £80

   C   £20

   D   £10

   Answer C

Comments
A Incorrect – this is the new value of the interest that it will have to pay.
B Incorrect – this is the value of the interest before the increase.
C Correct – this is the value of the increase £100 – £80.
D Incorrect – this would be interest charged at 1%.

2. A small car dealer, which buys and sells second hand cars, has £5,000 in the bank in savings and has no loans. Interest rates rise substantially. What is **most likely** to be the effect on this firm?

   Select **one** answer.

   A   It may be better off because its car sales are likely to rise and it will receive more interest on its savings

   B   It may be worse off because, although it will receive more interest on its savings, its car sales will fall

   C   It may be worse off because its car sales will fall and it will receive less interest on its savings

   D   It may be better off because its car sales will rise although it will receive less interest on its savings

   Answer B

Comments
A Incorrect – sales of cars will probably fall as credit becomes more expensive.
B Correct – it could lose more in profits than it gains from interest on the savings – depending on the extent to which sales are hit.
C Incorrect – it will receive more interest on its savings.
D Incorrect – sales of cars will probably fall as credit becomes more expensive and it will receive more in interest on the savings.

3. Most of the customers of a furniture shop buy items through borrowing the money. The furniture shop has an overdraft and a bank loan. Interest rates come down substantially. What is **most likely** to be the effect on the shop?

Select **one** answer.

A   Its sales will rise and it will pay more interest on its borrowings

B   Its sales will rise and it will pay less interest on its borrowings

C   Its sales will fall and it will pay more interest on its borrowings

D   Its sales will fall and it will pay less interest on its borrowings

Answer B

Comments
A Incorrect – it will pay **less** on its borrowings.
B Correct – consumers will be more confident and will buy more plus the interest on the overdraft will be less.
C Incorrect – sales will **rise** and it will pay **less** on its borrowings.
D Incorrect – sales will **rise**.

Chapter 25: **The impact of interest rates**

Twelve months ago, Cotgrove's was a thriving business. The small firm had three shops that sold electrical appliances such as televisions, games consoles, cookers and microwave ovens. The last shop had only recently opened. To finance the opening, Cotgrove's had borrowed £100,000 from its bank at a fixed rate of interest over 4 years. The repayments were £30,000 a year spread over the four years. Cotgrove's also had an overdraft facility of £30,000, which meant that it could become overdrawn on its current account at the bank by up to £30,000.

Since this time, the Bank of England has put up interest rates from 2.5 per cent to 6.0 per cent. It was worried about rising inflation in the economy. The rise in interest rates has had a dramatic impact on Cotgrove's. Sales have fallen by 20 per cent. The company has been left with all the costs of running three shops but with fewer customers buying its products. Its overdraft has risen as Cotgrove's has struggled to pay its day-to-day bills. The actual overdraft now stands at £27,000 and is still rising. To get some more cash flowing through the business, Cotgrove's has decided to run a sale offering large discounts on its stock of products.

1. Explain how a rise in interest rates has led to a fall in spending at Cotgrove's.   (3)

Indicative content

- Consumers have lower disposable income.

- Loans are now more expensive and consumers may put off buying these types of products.

- These types of products tend to be luxuries and so consumers may decide to cut back on spending of these items as they are not necessities.

- Lack of repeat purchases – consumers may decide to make do with their existing products rather than buy new ones.

Mark scheme

Up to 3 marks for the explanation. For example, higher interest rates make borrowing more expensive. (1 mark) If people have to pay back more they are likely to borrow less. (1 mark) If people have less to spend they may buy fewer goods on credit, such as the electrical goods at Cotgrove's. (1 mark)

2. Using examples, show how Cotgrove's costs have been affected by the rise in interest rates. (3)

Indicative content

- Costs will rise and more to pay back

- Increase in the rate means higher percentage paid which increases the amount paid.

- Suitable numerical example.

Mark scheme

If interest rates go up then the amount that has to be paid back to the bank will go up. (1 mark) For example, an increase from 2.5% to 6.0% will increase the repayments on an overdraft of £27,000 from £675 to £1,620 each year. (1 mark) Increased payments on borrowing by Cotgrove's will mean that its costs have gone up. (1 mark)

3. Discuss whether or not the sale will help solve Cotgrove's problems in both the short term and the long term. (9)

Indicative content

Help

- Bring new customer base
- Improve cash flow
- Reduce overdraft
- Reduce interest on overdraft
- Lowers costs

Not help

- Prices will go back up
- Are enough new customers attracted or debts reduced?
- May need to restructure finance – better credit control, reducing costs
- May hide real problems

Mark scheme

Level	Mark	Descriptor
	No mark	Non-rewardable material
Level 1	1–3	A choice will be made with poorly developed justification and supported by limited examples. For example, 'No, customers will buy more, but this will not last.'
Level 2	4–6	A choice will be made with some developed justification and supported by some good examples and some balance to the answer. For example, 'No. Reducing prices in a sale will encourage customers to spend more. But this will only be for the period of the sale. If prices rise then spending may fall again. This is not a long-term solution but will lead to some short-term benefit.'
Level 3	7–9	A choice will be made with a clearly developed justification and supported by excellent examples. The answer will be well balanced and will reach conclusion relating to both the short term and the long term. For example, 'The business must consider whether a sale will solve its problems in the long-term. A sale may encourage people to spend in the short-term. New customers may be attracted to the shop and it may improve cash flow and allow some of the borrowing to be paid off. But in the longer term prices are likely to rise again. Spending may fall again as a result. Unless the sales has attracted large enough numbers to continue to buy or enough debts have been repaid this will not solve the real problems of the business.'

4. Evaluate whether Cotgrove should close one of its shops to solve its problems. (6)

Indicative content

Will depend on a variety of factors

- Which one
- Size of saving
- May lose customers
- What will happen to its reputation
- Customer confidence may be dented
- How far will it reduce overheads
- Does not affect loan repayments so may have limited effect
- May reduce overdraft
- It may help to cut costs but the business will also have to think about the future and what will happen to interest rates

Mark scheme

Level	Mark	Descriptor
	No mark	Non-rewardable material
Level 1	1–2	A choice will be made with poorly developed justification and supported by limited examples. For example, 'Yes. The money it saves can reduce its borrowing.'
Level 2	3–4	A choice will be made with some developed justification and supported by some good examples. For example, 'Yes. The business may lose some revenue from the shop because it is now not selling any items as a result of the closure. But closing the shop will reduce its costs and may leave it in a better financial position.'
Level 3	5–6	A choice will be made with a clearly developed justification and supported by excellent examples. The answer will have some balance. For example, 'The business must evaluate the costs and benefits of closing one shop. One the one hand it will lose revenue and its reputation may be affected. Also, the rise in interest rates may only be for a short term. However, the business does appear to have longer term problems. It may need to close the shop to cut costs and also pay off its borrowing. This may leave it in a better position, as a smaller, leaner but more effective operation. If the benefits outweigh the costs then they should close it.'

Chapter 25: **The impact of interest rates**

1   What is meant by the term 'interest rate'?

2   What is meant by the term 'variable interest rates'?

3   What is meant by the term 'fixed interest rates'?

4   A business has a loan with a fixed interest rate. How would a fall in the interest rate affect its cash flow?

5   If a business had a mortgage with a variable interest rate, how would a rise in the interest rate affect its cash flow?

6   How would a fall in interest rates affect someone with a savings account?

7   State two ways in which a rise in interest rates could affect a homeowner with a mortgage that has a variable interest rate.

Ciaran Osume runs a business selling second hand caravans. He is always at the limit of his overdraft of £100,000 and he pays a variable interest rate on it. He arranges loans for people who want one to buy a caravan.

8   If interest rates go up by 2%, by how much will Ciaran's payments change if he is at the limit of his overdraft?

9   State two ways that Ciaran might react to this.

10 How might the change in interest rates affect demand for his caravans from customers?

Suggested answers

1 Interest rates are the percentage charged on a loan taken out by borrowers or the reward earned by savers.

2 Variable interest rates are interest rates that change over the time of a loan and track the Base Rate set by the Bank of England.

3 Fixed interest rates are interest rates that stay the same over an agreed period of time and are agreed at the start.

4 It would have no effect as the rate is fixed and was agreed at the start of the loan.

5 The business would pay more interest on the mortgage, so monthly payments would rise. This would reduce cash flow as more money is flowing out of the business in payments.

6 A fall in interest rates would mean that savers would earn less money on their savings than before.

7 The homeowner would have to pay higher payments, so the money left over to spend would be less. With less money to spend homeowners would have to make choices about what to buy. Some products would not be purchased depending on how important they were to the buyer.

8 His costs will rise by £100,000 x 2% = £2,000 per year.

9 Ciaran could try to reduce his costs by paying off some of the overdraft, perhaps by selling off caravans cheaply. Or he could try to clear the debt and try to arrange another loan at a lower rate.

10 The rise in interest rates would be likely to cause demand for his caravans to fall. Caravans might be considered a luxury and consumers might decide to put off purchases of such expensive items. Loans to buy such items would be more expensive and this could put some buyers off, as their repayments would be greater. On the other hand some customers might sell their caravans and buy cheaper second hand caravans, which might increase demand.

Chapter 26: The impact of exchange rates

1. A small firm orders $6,000 worth of materials from a foreign supplier. If the exchange rate is £1 = $1.50, how much in £ will it have to pay for the order?

   Select **one** answer.

   A   £4,000

   B   £6,000

   C   £9,000

   D   £10,000

   Answer A

Comments
A Correct – To buy $6,000 the UK buyer would have to give up £4,000 (6,000/1.50 = 4,000).
B Incorrect – the exchange rate would then be £1 = $1.
C Incorrect – the exchange rate would then be £1 = $0.66.
D Incorrect – the exchange rate would then be £1 = $0.6.

2. A UK firm sells furniture and kitchen products to customers in Europe and buys raw materials from Germany. The value of the £ (pound sterling) falls sharply against the euro.

   The fall in the value of the £ is most likely to mean that

   A   its sales to customers in Europe will fall

   B   the cost of raw materials bought from Germany will fall

   C   it will export more to customers in Europe

   D   its total costs will fall

   Select **one** answer.

   Answer C

Comments
A Incorrect – sales should increase – a weaker pound means that foreign buyers have to give up less euros to get an amount of pounds.
B Incorrect – the cost will increase – the UK firm will have to give up more pounds to get the same amount of euro.
C Correct – UK goods will be relatively cheaper for people in Europe to buy – they will have to give up fewer euro to buy the same amount of pounds.
D Incorrect – total costs will be likely to rise as the variable costs of the raw materials go up.

3. The value of the pound (£) rises against other currencies. This is likely to

    A   increase exports of goods by UK firms

    B   make UK firms less competitive in foreign markets

    C   reduce imports of goods by UK firms

    D   make UK firms more competitive in the domestic market against imports into the UK

    Select **one** answer.

    Answer B

Comments
A Incorrect – exports will appear to be more expensive to foreign buyers so it is likely that sales abroad will fall.
B Correct – they will now appear expensive compared with products made in the home country.
C Incorrect – it will lead to an increase in imports as they appear cheaper – UK buyers have to give up fewer pounds to get the same amount of the foreign currency.
D Incorrect – they will be less competitive – imported goods will appear cheaper and this is likely to mean demand for imported goods will rise.

Chapter 26: **The impact of exchange rates**

Bishton's is a small food manufacturer based in Milton Keynes. It makes traditional English biscuits and cakes that it sells worldwide. It buys some of its ingredients from abroad.

Over the past six months, the value of the pound has fallen against the euro and the dollar. For example, whereas six months ago, £1 would buy 1.30 euro it now only buys 1.00 euro.

Bishton's has been pleased with the fall in the value of the pound. It is mounting an aggressive sales drive abroad to market its products. Lower prices are one of the key elements in this marketing initiative.

However, Bishton's costs have risen. In the short term, this has affected profits because it takes time for overseas sales to increase. Profits have also been affected because it has not increased its prices to UK customers. It sells 30 per cent of its output in the UK, all to shops and other retail outlets in tourist centres in the UK.

1. Bishton's buys 13,000 euro worth of raw materials from France. Using the exchange rates mentioned in the passage, calculate the **difference** in price in £ that it paid six months ago compared to today? Show your workings. (3)

Mark scheme

- Before 13,000 euro ÷1.3 = £10,000. (1 mark)

- After 13,000 euro ÷1.0 = £13,000. (1 mark)

- Therefore it paid £3,000 more. (1 mark)

2. The price of a pack of biscuits that Bishton's sell is £1.50. Explain what has happened to the change in the amount that its French customers will have to pay if the value of the pound changes from £1 = 1.30 euro to £1 = 1.00 euro. Show your workings. (3)

Mark scheme

At £1 = 1.30 euro, French buyers would have to pay 1.50 x 1.30 = 1.95 euro. (1 mark)

At £1 = 1.00 euro, French buyers would now have to pay 1.50 x 1.00 = 1.50 euro. (1 mark)

The price of a pack of biscuits will have appeared to have fallen by 45 cents to the French buyers. (1 mark)

3. Explain **two** reasons why Bishton's is 'mounting an aggressive sales drive abroad'. (6)

Indicative content

- Falling exchange rate makes them more competitive – chance to increase sales

- 70% of business is abroad – makes the effect of the exchange rate more significant

- Additional sales revenue, if generated, help pay for rising costs

- Mutual trade with countries supplying raw materials

- Competition at home might mean that it needs to seek opportunities abroad

- Cannot pass on price increases so falling profits – needs the additional revenue

- May wish to exploit USP (English product/image)

Over to you answers
Topic 1.5: The economic context
BUSINESS

Mark scheme

Up to 3 marks for explanation of each reason. For example, 'They may be seeking to increase sales abroad to compensate for falling profits. (1 mark) Costs are rising, but the business is unable to increase its prices in the UK to cover them and profits have fallen as a result. (1 mark) Marketing into Europe, helped by a falling exchange rate, may help it to increase its sales and profits. (1 mark)

4.   Do you think the fall in the value of the pound will benefit Bishton's or harm the business? Justify your answer.   (6)

Indicative content

Benefit

- 70% of business is abroad
- USP (English product/ image)
- Wider customer base
- Exports more than it imports

Harm

- Costs of imports rises
- Depends where imports come from, US or Europe
- Proportion of variable costs to total costs
- May be ignoring 30% of market

Mark scheme

Level	Mark	Descriptor
	No mark	Non-rewardable material
Level 1	1–2	A choice will be made with poorly developed justification and supported by limited examples. For example, 'It should benefit the business. A fall in the exchange rate should lead to increased exports.'
Level 2	3–4	A choice will be made with some developed justification and supported by some good examples with some balance offered at the top end of the mark range. For example, 'It should benefit the business. The prices of only some of the ingredients it buys from abroad will go up, as a fall in the exchange rate raises import prices. But export prices will fall as the value of the pound falls. So it should be able to increase sales abroad.'
Level 3	5–6	A choice will be made with a clearly developed justification and supported by excellent examples. The balance will be clear and a conclusion will be given to pull the answer together. For example, 'The business should benefit. Although it buys some ingredients from abroad and will have to pay higher import prices, it sells the vast majority of its products abroad. The fall in the exchange rate should mean that it will be able to increase sales – supported by the aggressive marketing campaign. This may have the effect of increasing revenue to more than balance out the increase in costs. The passage does say that the company is 'pleased with the fall in the exchange rate' which suggests they believe it will bring greater benefits than costs. As a result the evidence would suggest a net benefit to the business of the fall in the exchange rate.'

Chapter 26: **The impact of exchange rates**

1   What is meant by the term 'exchange rate'?

2   What is meant by the term 'export'?

3   What is meant by the term 'import'?

4   Explain the phrase 'strong pound against the euro (€)'.

5   Explain the phrase 'a falling value of the pound against the dollar' using an example.

A UK clothing business exports £1,000 worth of products to France. The value of the pound rises from £1 = €1.20 to €1.30.

6   How much would the French buyers have to pay in euro before the change? How much would they have to pay after the change?

7   What is likely to happen to exports of clothing?

If the value of the pound falls from £1 =$2 to £1 = $1.5 what would be the effect on the following businesses?

8   A perfume maker which exports **most** of its products to the USA.

9   A biscuit manufacturer that imports **most** of its raw materials from the USA.

10 Demand for French designer clothes.

Suggested answers

1 The exchange rate is the price of buying a foreign currency – how much of one currency you have to give up to buy or acquire an amount of another currency.

2 A product sold abroad and which leads to money flowing into a country.

3 A product bought from abroad and which leads to money flowing out of a country.

4 This when the pound buys more euro than at other times – the buyer gets more euro for every pound they give up.

5 This is where the pound buys fewer dollars than before. An example would be if the value of the pound fell from £1 = $1.50 to £1 = $1.20. In this example, the buyer would now only get $1.20 for every pound given up compared to $1.50 before the change in the exchange rate.

6 Before the change the clothing costs £1,000 x 1.20 = €1,200. After the change the clothing costs £1,000 x 1.30 = €1,300.

7 French buyers now have to give up more euro to get the same amount of pounds so it appears to them that the price has risen. Exports of clothing are likely to fall, therefore, because of the higher price.

8 Because the pound is weaker than the dollar, US buyers would have to give up fewer dollars to acquire the pounds they need to buy the perfume exports, so the perfume would seem cheaper than before. This means demand for exports is likely to rise and more perfume is likely to be sold. As a result revenue and profit for the perfume maker is likely to increase.

9 Because the pound is weaker, the biscuit manufacturer will have to give up more pounds to buy the same amount of dollars and so will pay more for the imports. This will increase its costs when making the biscuits. It may have to put the price up to maintain profits, but this might affect sales revenue. Its biscuits will seem more expensive than biscuits made using UK materials. Whether demand falls will depend on how sensitive it is to price changes.

10 There will be no change in demand because the pound has altered against the dollar not the euro.

Chapter 27: **The impact of the business cycle**

1. Cremin's is an independent shop selling records, CDs and DVDs. It has decided to open a second store in a nearby area of London. Which **one** of the following is most likely to be the reason why it has decided to expand?

    Select **one** answer.

    A   Interest rates are at record high levels

    B   The economy is growing very fast

    C   Competition from internet retailers of records, CDs and DVDs is getting more intense

    D   Rents on shops are very high

    Answer B

Comments
A Incorrect – this would discourage them as a loan would be expensive.
B Correct – demand is going up and consumers have more money to spend.
C Incorrect – this would suggest they should not open a new shop.
D Incorrect – this would put them off as fixed costs would be high.

2. Agaba's is a restaurant. The economy is doing badly at the moment, incomes are falling and unemployment is rising. Agaba's has seen a drop in sales too. Which **one** of the following is most likely to help Agaba's survive?

    It should

    A   take on an extra worker

    B   buy another local loss-making restaurant

    C   introduce a take-away service

    D   increase the pay of the owners of the restaurant

    Select **one** answer.

    Answer C

Comments
A Incorrect – this will add to their costs and make things worse.
B Incorrect – this will add to their costs and make things worse.
C Correct – by changing the product they can possibly gain new customers and extra revenue.
D Incorrect – this will add to their costs and make things worse.

3. Dineley's is a small taxi firm. It has decided to sell one of its taxis. Which **one** of the following is the most likely reason for this? Over the past twelve months

   A   the level of economic activity in the economy has fallen

   B   the price of diesel has fallen

   C   another local taxi firm has closed

   D   the price of second hand cars has fallen

Select **one** answer.

Answer A

Comments
A Correct – demand for taxi rides is likely to have fallen if customers' incomes have fallen.
B Incorrect – this is not relevant.
C Incorrect – it's likely they would need more taxis to take up the extra demand.
D Incorrect – it might affect the price they get for their taxi but is not a reason why it has decided to sell the taxi.

Chapter 27: **The impact of the business cycle**

Gisborne's is a small firm which supplies spare parts for diggers used in construction and road building. It buys stocks from major manufacturers and then sells them to businesses that own diggers.

Twelve months ago, the firm was doing well and had achieved the highest sales ever in its four year history. It had expanded the number of parts it kept in stock to cope with higher sales and taken on an extra member of staff. It had also moved to larger premises, taking out a large loan to pay for the move.

However, the past twelve months have been very bad for Gisborne's. The level of economic activity has fallen dramatically and the economy has gone into recession. As the business cycle has changed, economic growth has fallen by 2 per cent. The construction industry has been particularly badly affected with sales falling by 25 per cent. This means that there are now a lot of diggers lying idle in builder's yards that do not need any replacement parts. The only good thing is that construction companies have stopped buying new diggers. They have been making do with the diggers they already own. Older machines break down more frequently and so need more parts. Even so, Gisborne's has seen its sales fall by 20 per cent.

1. Explain what is meant by the business cycle. (3)

Indicative content

- Fluctuations in business activity
- Different elements – growth, downturn, recession, recovery
- Demand change – less buying means a fall in economic activity
- Consumer confidence changes during different times in the cycle
- Economic activity changes over time – sometimes it is rising and at other times it slows down.

Mark scheme

Up to 3 marks for explanation. For example, 'The business cycle shows the fluctuations in the level of economic activity over a period of time. (1 mark) Most economies go through periods when the economy is growing, to be followed by times when the level of economic activity slows down. (1 mark) Conditions are different at different stages. For example, in a growth period consumer spending is rising and confidence is high, but in a downturn consumer spending is falling and confidence is low'. (1 mark)

2. Explain the likely impact that the change in the level of economic activity over the past 12 months is having on Gisborne's. In your answer, analyse the likely impact on revenues, costs and profits. (6)

Indicative content

- Revenue high 12 months ago but sales have now fallen
- Still have customers, as parts are still needed
- Costs increased as a result of larger premises, loans, more staff and stock
- Profits falling

Mark scheme

The marks will be awarded for the links made in the analysis. The question asks for the effect on revenues, costs and profits to be considered. It is expected that some reference should be made to economic activity with the analysis showing the links between the change in activity and the effect on the different aspects of the business. For example, 'The slowdown in economic activity means that the amount of buying and selling in the economy goes down (1 mark). Sales at Gisborne's were at a peak 12 months ago, but fell by 20% cent over the period because of the slowdown. Sales revenue will have fallen as a result. (1 mark) The fall in sales was reduced to some extent by demand for spare parts. (1 mark) Fixed costs increased as the business moved to larger premises, including paying interest on a loan. (1 mark) Variable costs also increased as the business built up stock. (1 mark) Lower sales revenue and higher costs will have led to fall in profit.' (1 mark)

3. Explain how making a worker redundant might help Gisborne's during a slowdown. (3)

Indicative content

- Reduce costs/overheads via wages
- Reduce taxes to government (NICs)
- Improves cash flow
- Offsets cuts in revenue
- May help to limit the loss the company might make or help to maintain profit levels
- Money saved on wages can be used to help pay other essential costs

Mark scheme

Up to 3 marks for explanation. For example, 'Making a worker redundant could contribute to reducing the cost of paying wages and National Insurance contributions. (1 mark) If costs fall then the business can use the money it would have paid in wage costs to pay off its loan. (1 mark) Or it may be used to compensate for falling sales and maintain profit until the economy recovers and sales pick up.' (1 mark)

4. Compare **two** different measures that Gisborne's might take to survive the slowdown apart from making workers redundant. Discuss which **one** you think could be the most important in ensuring its survival. (9)

Indicative content

Sell off premises

- Reduce outgoings
- Pay off loan
- One-off action
- Depends on how much it raises
- May need other strategies alongside

Reduce prices

- May increase revenue – profits may fall or rise depending on response
- May be no reaction from customers to the price reduction so might not work
- Short-term measure
- New customers may be generated as a result
- Might possibly help it to increase market share

Restructure finance

- Increase its overdraft to meet changed cash flow situation
- Try to find ways to reduce its outgoings – its fixed and variable costs
- Try to renegotiate the terms of its loan with its bank – maybe pay it off over a longer period of time
- Be willing to accept lower profits during the slowdown
- Find ways to make sure it gets the payments it is owed by debtors

Find new customers

- Carry out market research to find new customers
- Look to promote their product and service more effectively

Over to you answers
Topic 1.5: The economic context
BUSINESS

Mark scheme

Level	Mark	Descriptor
	No mark	Non-rewardable material
Level 1	1–3	Up to two measures are given but with limited development of one or both. At the top of the mark range a judgement is given but not supported. For example, 'Two methods could be selling property and restructuring finance. Reducing costs such as loans could be the easiest method.'
Level 2	4–6	Up to two measures are given with some development of each and some attempt to draw a comparison. At the top end of the mark range a judgement will also be given with some limited support. For example, 'Two methods could be reducing their prices and restructuring finance. Reducing prices might help to encourage more sales. Restructuring its finance may mean getting an extension to its overdraft to help it manage its cash flow. Given that Gisborne's is facing a slowdown and sales in construction have fallen so far, it is probably better to try to get an overdraft extension because even if it does reduce prices there may not be the business available to get more sales.'
Level 3	7–9	Two measures are given with some analysis of each which makes use of appropriate terminology. There is a clear attempt to draw a comparison and a conclusion will be given that makes a judgement and draws together the analysis given.
		For example, 'Two ways to cope with the slowdown is to restructure its finance and find new customers. It can try to negotiate new terms for its loan with its bank to try and pay the loan back over a longer period of time and reduce its monthly payments. This will help reduce its costs. As its cash flow is weaker it might also ask for an extension of its overdraft to help cover the weaker cash flow. It could try to find ways of finding new customers. This could be done by some market research. However, this is likely to be expensive and may not be appropriate given the economic conditions. As the construction industry has slowed down quite a lot there may simply not be any new customers anyway.
		As a result it would seem that dealing with its finance may be a better way of surviving the slowdown. It is not in a totally hopeless situation as firms are repairing diggers rather than buying new ones so it might benefit from that. It can explain this to the bank that may be willing to take the risk of helping with finance. Restructuring finance will be the most appropriate option, therefore.'

Chapter 27: **The impact of the business cycle**

1 What is meant by the term 'economic activity'?

2 What is meant by the term 'economic growth'?

3 What is meant by the term 'economic slowdown'?

4 What is meant by the term 'recession'?

5 Explain the term 'business cycle'.

6 State two features of a recession.

7 State two reasons why people may feel more confident in a period of growth.

8 Explain how a recession abroad can affect UK export businesses.

9 Explain how rising unemployment might add to the problems in a recession.

10 Explain how offering 0% by a business on loans for goods might help economic growth.

Suggested answers

1 Economic activity is the amount of buying and selling that goes on in an economy over time.

2 Economic growth is when there is a rise in the level of economic activity so more goods and services are being bought and sold (more buying and selling).

3 An economic slowdown is where the rate of growth starts to slow down – the amount of buying and selling starts to slow down.

4 A recession is when economic growth is negative over two or more successive quarters.

5 The business cycle is the pattern by which economic activity changes over time. When more is being bought and sold the economy is said to be growing and when less is being sold it is said to be slowing down. The pattern tends to be repeated over time, with some periods of growth followed by periods of slower growth or possible recession.

6 Features of recession include less likelihood of large wage increases, reduced or more cautious spending, low consumer and business confidence, low growth, high unemployment and higher rates of business failure.

7 Reasons might include job security, high wage rises and businesses doing well.

8 The effect of recession abroad may be felt by businesses that rely mainly on exports for their income. If there is recession then fewer of their goods and services will needed by foreign buyers. The businesses may then have to lay off staff as they have less work to be done and also feel less confident about the prospects for future sales.

9 Unemployment is often a feature of recession but then it adds to it. This is because if people become unemployed their incomes fall and families have to be more selective about what they buy. It could be they switch to more own label goods or stop buying some products at all. In turn this means shops' turnover falls so they need fewer staff and need to buy in fewer goods. The whole situation becomes a downward spiral as one part fuels the other.

10 Offering 0% interest means that people are not being charged interest on payments over a period of time. Often businesses charge interest on payments spread over time in the same way that banks charge interest on loans (the two are in effect the same thing). Offering interest free payments might make the products relatively cheaper and encourage people to buy goods they might not have bought. It might also encourage people to buy more expensive goods that they can only afford by spreading payments. This spending might help the economy to grow.

Chapter 28: Business decisions and stakeholders

1. Cantwell's is a business that makes zips for clothing. It decides to make five workers redundant. Which **one** of the following is most likely to benefit from this decision?

   Select **one** answer.

   A Suppliers of the business because they will now sell more zips to Cantwell's

   B The local community because there will now be more spending in local shops

   C The government because it will now collect more in tax

   D The owners because their costs will fall

   Answer D

Comments
A Incorrect – this is unlikely to have any direct effect on them.
B Incorrect – it's likely there will be less spending as workers have less money when they are unemployed.
C Incorrect – it will collect less tax – if workers are not working they pay no income tax.
D Correct – they will pay less in wages.

2. Bettany's is a business that makes wire trolleys for supermarkets. It has decided to invest in a new machine and take on two more workers because orders are increasing. Which stakeholder in the company is most likely to benefit by the decision?

   Select **one** answer.

   A Owners because increasing sales means their total costs will fall

   B Workers because their jobs will now be more secure

   C Supermarkets because the price of wire trolleys will increase

   D The government because it will now collect less in tax

   Answer B

Comments
A Incorrect – costs will rise as more products are made for sale – this is not a benefit.
B Correct – demand is increasing and the business is growing.
C Incorrect – this would be a drawback to Bettany's customers (the supermarkets). This is not a benefit.
D Incorrect – the government will collect more tax. This is not a benefit.

3. Sangar's is a small meat packing business. Its workers have demanded a 10 per cent pay rise. Which stakeholder in the company is most likely to be affected if the company awards the pay rise in full?

    Select **one** answer.

    A   Suppliers to Sangar's that will see a rise in sales to the company

    B   Customers who will see a fall in price of the products made by Sangar's

    C   The owners who will see the costs of the company rise

    D   The local community that will see a fall in spending in local shops

Answer C

Comments
A Incorrect – it's not relevant to them.
B Incorrect – the prices are likely to go up to cover the increased costs.
C Correct – wages are a cost to the company.
D Incorrect – spending will probably increase as workers have more money.

Chapter 28: Business decisions and stakeholders

Manian's Ltd is a small company which provides a repairs and maintenance service for commercial and residential property. Most of their work comes through maintenance agreements. The owners of a building, like an office block or a block of flats, sign a maintenance agreement with Manian's. In return, Manian's guarantees a 24-hour, 365 days a year call out service. Manian's employs a team of 12 electricians, plumbers, carpenters and decorators to do its work. It also hires extra workers by the day if it is very busy.

A typical job might be a leak in a pipe. A plumber will be sent out to fix the leak. If it is serious enough, it might need a carpenter to repair damaged woodwork or refix a ceiling. A serious leak is also likely to have damaged wall and ceiling decoration. So the company's decorators will be sent out to redecorate.

The company prides itself on getting work done quickly. It also aims to provide a one-stop service. The owners of the building do not have to look for more builders to do day to day repair and maintenance work. If there is a job that is beyond the expertise of Manian's workers, like a difficult repair job to a boiler, Manian's will organise a company to come and fix the problem immediately. Outside maintenance of a building is just as important as inside. Having a well kept outside deters burglars and enhances the look of the local area. It also helps maintain the value of the property, particularly important if the customer is a group of flat owners in a complex of flats.

Manian's is owned by Fred Mansell and Brian Simister. They both had long experience in the building trade before setting up the company. They see quality of work and speed of response as key to running a successful company. They have seen their sales and their profits grow substantially since setting up the company five years ago. They hope that by the time they retire, they will have established a business that will be worth several million pounds to a buyer.

1. Explain the interest that each of the following stakeholders has in Manian's.

    (a) Fred Mansell and Brian Simister

    (b) the 12 employees of Manian's

    (c) the customer's of Manian's

    (d) the local community. (12)

Indicative content
(a)
- Owners
- Profit
- Shareholders
- Pension
- Business to sell on

(b)
- Employment
- Wages
- Job security
- Taxes paid
- Working conditions

Over to you answers
Topic 1.5: The economic context
BUSINESS

(c)

- Product (service)
- Value for money
- Customer service/after sales service
- Confidence
- Security
- Peace of mind

(d)

- Employment
- Appearance
- Reputation/image
- Crime
- Value of **all** properties

Mark scheme

Up to a maximum of 3 marks for an explanation of each stakeholder interest (a-d). For example, 'Fred Mansell and Brain Simister are the owners of the business. They are directly affected by its activities. (1 mark) If the business does well and makes a profit then they may benefit. (1 mark) For example, they may be able to take profit from the business for themselves as owners and will also benefit when the company is sold as a profitable company should sell for a good price.'

2. Manian's decides to put up the prices of its maintenance contracts by 4 per cent to reflect increases in costs, including a pay rise to its workers. Explain what impact this might have on **two** different stakeholders in the company. (6)

Indicative content

Owners

- Profit

Customers

- May have to pass on the increase in costs as rent increases
- May not be happy with the price increase
- Might decide to cancel the contract
- May feel that the price rise is OK as Manian's provides value for money

Workers

- Increase in wages will be seen as a benefit
- May improve their happiness at work
- May feel more secure and valued

Government

- Increased tax revenue as workers' incomes have increased and so income tax payments will rise

Community

- May not worry if Manian's continue to provide a good service
- Some local businesses may benefit from increased spending of workers

Conflicting objectives

- Customers – having to pay higher prices (may not be happy)
- Workers – pleased to get a pay rise

Mark scheme

Up to 3 marks for explanation of how each stakeholder will be affected. For example, 'If it puts up its prices then customers may face higher prices. (1 mark) they will have to pay more for the services and may feel unhappy that they are getting the same service for a higher price and may think they are getting less value for money. (1 mark) Some customers may start to search around for cheaper alternatives, although loyal customers may be prepared to pay the higher price for the quality of the service the business provides.' (1 mark)

3. Fred Mansell and Brian Simister decide they could increase the profitability of the company if they made two workers redundant and hired more temporary workers when work was busy. Discuss whether this is in the best interests of customers and the owners of the business.   (6)

Indicative content

Owners

*   Reduced costs.
*   More profit.
*   More flexibility.
*   Will depend on the balance between the cost savings they get and the effect on the quality of work that gets done.
*   If benefit of cost savings are less than the cost of loss of reputation and increases in complaints about quality it may not be worth doing.

Customers

*   After sales service may be worse.
*   Value for money – may result in lower prices.
*   If the cost of providing the service does not rise then it might be that their rents will not change.
*   Will depend on the level of service they will get – if no change then may be quite happy.

Mark scheme

Level	Mark	Descriptor
	No mark	Non-rewardable material
Level 1	1–2	A judgement will be made with reference to one stakeholder with some limited development. For example, 'It's in the best interest of owners because they will make more profit.'
Level 2	3–4	A judgement will be made with reference to both Stakeholders, along with some limited development of each. For example, 'The owners will benefit because they will be able to be more flexible in the way they run their business but the customers may not be happy because it might mean they will have a poorer service if there are only temporary workers being used.'
Level 3	5–6	A judgement is made referring to both stakeholders with some well reasoned development of both and using appropriate terminology. A conclusion is drawn in relation to the analysis provided. For example, 'The owners will be able to reduce their labour costs if they make two workers redundant. Customers may be concerned that the quality of the work that gets done might not be as good or as prompt. This will also be a concern of the owners and they will have to be sure that the benefits they get from reducing their costs are not outweighed by the disadvantages that might arise from customers being unhappy with the new service. If the owners can make sure that the temporary workers are of the right standard and have the right training then both customers and owners could benefit from the move as costs can be reduced and the quality of the service maintained.'

Chapter 28: Business decisions and stakeholders

1   What is meant by the term 'stakeholder'?

2   List four examples of stakeholders of a nightclub.

3   Stakeholders are sometimes said to have 'conflicting interests'. What does a conflict of interest mean?

A supermarket claims there has been a 20% increase in its online grocery shopping, mainly to small villages. How might this affect the following stakeholders?

4   Workers in the supermarket.

5   Competitors.

6   Residents in a small village.

7   Suppliers.

8   Shareholders in the supermarket.

9   The Government.

10 Explain how the supermarket could try and meet the demands of all its stakeholders.

Suggested answers

1 A stakeholder is someone who has an interest in the progress of a business and the effects that progress will have on them.

2 Stakeholders in the night club might be the owners, local residents affected by the noise, clubbers (customers) who visit the club, the Government which receives tax from the club, suppliers of drinks to the club or artists who perform at the club.

3 A conflict of interest is a situation where benefits from a business decision bring benefits to one stakeholder but cause a drawback or disadvantage to another. So the decision is welcomed by one stakeholder group but is disliked by another.

4 There would be different views. There may be fewer workers needed at the supermarket so they would be unhappy. On the other hand more drivers would be needed, so they would be happy.

5 They would be unhappy as it is likely the increase means they are losing business to the supermarket. Their revenue would fall and they would lose profits.

6 Some of the residents would be happy because they are getting a better service and probably better prices. Some might be unhappy if there was a lot of congestion, noise and air pollution caused by more and bigger lorries delivering.

7 They would be happy because there would be more demand for their products they supply to the supermarket.

8 They would be happy because more sales should mean more profits (assuming costs do not rise by the same amount). If profits go up then their share of the profits goes up, too.

9 The government would be happy because if more is being sold then they collect more tax from VAT, and more corporation tax, income tax and NICs from the businesses and from workers. If more workers are needed to meet the increase in demand then the government will pay out less in benefits.

10 The supermarket could offer training courses for any workers who may be made redundant or offer them jobs in other parts of the business if more online business means less work in the supermarket itself. They could agree to deliver only at certain times of the day so that would assist those village residents who are fed up with constant noise. They would not care about competitors. The supermarket would need to ensure that more online business did not lead to smaller profits so that shareholders suffered. It would need to ensure the online business was extra business, not just a switch. Despite these steps it might find that it creates conflicts elsewhere, but there will never be a way in which all stakeholders can be totally satisfied. It is a delicate balancing act.

Practice exam questions

Claire Graham is a furniture designer and an entrepreneur. She saw a market for her speciality furniture, took the opportunity and set up her company called 'C-scapes Ltd'. She needed specialist equipment, premises and well qualified staff as her products were expensive and often made to order. The price reflects an added value of 20%. Most raw materials were imported from Europe as Claire could not get them in the UK. The economy was growing, so Claire took out loans to buy the equipment, a mortgage to buy the premises and she arranged an overdraft facility to help the company if there were cash flow problems in the early days of trading. Most of the 'C-scapes Ltd' customers were based in the UK, though they did export a few items to Europe. Claire was careful in how she ran 'C-scapes Ltd' and being aware of how economic activity could change she ensured that most of the profits were kept in the company so that it always had cash available. After two years interest rates rose and the value of the pound fell against the euro. There was a downturn in the economy as growth slowed.

(a) Which **two** of the following are **most likely** to exist in a growing economy? (2)

    A   The value of goods and services produced is going down

    B   Consumer confidence is low

    C   The standard of living is going up

    D   Incomes are going down

    E   Employment is rising

    F   There is less competition

Answer C and E

Examiner's comment

A Incorrect –this describes an economy in a downturn.

B Incorrect – this is what you would expect to see when the economy is in a downturn.

C Correct – more people have access to more goods and services when the economy is growing.

D Incorrect – in a growing economy you would expect incomes to rise not fall.

E Correct – when the economy is growing more goods and services are being produced so there are more people needed to produce them.

F Incorrect – in a growing economy there are more businesses opening up so you would expect to see more competition.

(b) (i) What is meant by the phrase 'a fall in the value of the pound'? (1)

(ii) Explain **one way** in which a fall in the value of the pound might affect C-scapes. (3)

Indicative content

(i)   A fall in value of the pound is where less foreign currency can be exchanged for a particular amount of pounds.

(ii)

- Imports may be more expensive.
- Raw materials more expensive.
- Costs might rise affecting profit.
- May have to look for new sources of raw materials.
- May have to consider increasing price to cover the rise in costs.
- May be able to sell more at home as there is less competition from other imports.
- Could benefit as she is more competitive abroad – export prices appear to have fallen to foreign buyers.
- May sell more abroad. How much more they sell may depend upon:
    – size of the fall in the value of the pound
    – how much demand would change when export prices fall.

Mark scheme

1 mark for explaining the phrase. For example, a fall in the value of the pound means that less foreign currency can be exchanged for a particular amount of pounds. An example would be if the value of the pound fell from £1 = 1.5 euros to £1 = 1 euro. (1 mark)

Up to 3 further marks for explanation of how this could affect C-scapes in one way. For example, a fall in the value of the pound against the euro will lead to a rise in the prices of raw material imports from Europe. (1 mark) If import prices rise, then the prices of raw material costs of C-scapes will rise. (1 mark) If they do not pass on the extra cost as higher prices this might affect their profit. (1 mark)

(c) Evaluate **one** likely effect on **two** stakeholders of your choice in C-scapes of the downturn in the economy. (6)

Indicative content

- Demand in the home market may fall
- Employees may feel their jobs are at risk
- The fact that she has been cautious with her money may mean the business can survive
- Banks may lose confidence and be more cautious in lending to businesses
- Specialised demand for her product so may not be as affected
- Export market might counterbalance – things may not be as bad abroad and so she could pick up sales abroad
- Claire is a private limited company – if the business did have to close she only risks losing her investment
- May have a limited effect – if she chooses to reduce prices she may maintain sales and still make a profit.

Mark scheme

Level	Mark	Descriptor
	No mark	Non-rewardable material
Level 1	1–2	A general description of what a downturn is with no reference to context or to stakeholders, For example, 'A downturn is when the economy stops growing and people don't buy as much'.
Level 2	3–4	A description of downturn would be made, two stakeholders would be identified and some basic comments made relating the two. For example, 'A downturn means there is less being spent and so stakeholders like the workers could be in danger of losing their jobs.' Or 'a downturn is when growth slows down and people lose confidence. The bank is a stakeholder in C-scapes and it might be worried that they cannot pay back the loans they took out. Or 'the economy might be slowing down so the business will not make as much profit. Claire and other shareholders will not get as much paid out to them and they might be unhappy.'
Level 3	5–6	The answer will refer to two stakeholders and offer some evaluative comment about the extent of the effect on each. For example, 'The economy will be slowing down and the workforce may be worried about jobs. However, if customers are still happy with the product and can afford it then there will be no problems. Claire might have to reduce profit margins but they would still be solvent.' Or 'a slowdown in the economy (downturn) means less might be demanded, so there would be less revenue. The bank might be worried but given that Claire has kept enough profits then they should be able to keep going. It is unlikely therefore that the downturn will affect her too badly but it depends on the size of the downturn.'

Edexcel scheme of work for Unit 1 Introduction to Small Business (28 weeks teaching)

Key to resources:
Pearson/Edexcel Student Book, Introduction to Small Business, Anderton, Gunn, Ashwin: 978-1-84690-496-7
Pearson Edexcel ActiveTeach: 978-1-84690-495-0
GCSE Business Studies Bitesize Revision – http://www.bbc.co.uk/schools/gcsebitesize/
Edexcel e-Bus resources - subscribed e-mail newsletter with Business Studies resources
Business case studies – GCSE Business Studies – M Hancock – Pearson: 978-1-4058-6447-3

Week	Content coverage/ key questions	Learning outcomes	Exemplar activities	Exemplar resources
1	**Topic 1.1 Spotting a business opportunity** What is a business?	To be able to state what a business does.	- Introductory activity to **debate** and **discuss** issues about 'Spotting a business opportunity'. 1 - Case study on a business giving motorcycle lessons – **explaining** the nature of business, its resources, its customers and **evaluating** why it might be successful. 1 - Interactive activity to help **understand** important terms in a business, such as 'market' and 'supplier'. 2 - A series of resources looking at what businesses do. For example, **discuss** what different businesses actually produce using photographs. 3	1 Student Book. Introduction to Small Business – Chapter 1 2 Active Teach 3 Introduction to Business Activity – Biz/ed: http://www.bized.co.uk/educators/level2/busactiv/ity/lesson/intro1.htm 3
2	Understanding customer needs.	To state why customer needs are central to a business.	- Case study on a cake making business, **explaining** how the business used market research and **evaluating** whether this was successful. 1 - Interactive activity **identifying** different types of market research using images. 2 - **Investigate** market research figures produced by a business and **explain** what they show. 3 - **Discuss** customer needs using case studies. 4	1 Student Book. Introduction to Small Business – Chapter 2 2 Active Teach 3 Business case studies – Case Study 14 – Market Research. 4 e-Bus: Sept 2006 – Heelys; Feb 2007 – Look investigation; March 2007 – Reggae lesson starter.

#	Topic	Learning objectives	Activities	Resources
3	**Topic 1.1 Spotting a business opportunity** Analysing customers.	To be able to identify your customers. To understand the types of customers that are being targeted. To understand the position of a business in order to spot a gap in the market.	- Case study on a hair stylist to **explain** how a business can use market mapping to identify target customers and whether there is a gap in the market, and to **evaluate** whether this will help the business to be successful. 1 - Students choose different brands within a product range and **construct** a market map related to price and quality. 4 - **Analyse** the position of different businesses on a market map. 2 - A series of resources looking at customers and market segments. For example, use the Yellow Pages or a Thomson Local Directory for your area to **identify** 20 different businesses and write down what type of customers these businesses might have. Also, **match** market segments with types of business using photographs and examples. 3	1 Student Book, Introduction to Small Business – Chapter 3 2 Active Teach 3 Knowing your customers – Biz/ed: http://www.bized.co.uk/educators/level2/competition/lesson/customers1.htm 4 Business Active: Volume 3 Number 2. Spring 2008. What's the use of branding? Market mapping task.
4	**Topic 1.1 Spotting a business opportunity** Analysing competitors.	To be able to recognise the importance of competitors in business planning. To be able to state at least 3 potential strengths and 3 weaknesses of competitors that might affect business planning.	- Case study on a gym to **identify** and **evaluate** its strengths and weaknesses. 1 - Interactive activity to **explain** the strengths and weaknesses of a taxi service **compared** to its competitors. 2 - **Examine** how strong brands can benefit competitors. 3	1 Student Book, Introduction to Small Business – Chapter 4 2 Active Teach 3 Business Active: Volume 3 Number 2. Spring 2008. What's the use of branding? pp 10 – 12.
5	**Topic 1.1 Spotting a business opportunity** Adding value.	To understand the meaning of the term 'added value'. To be able to recognise added value in three examples of products.	- Case study on a garage to **identify** how a business adds value, whether it has a USP and **evaluate** whether that USP will make the business successful. 1 - Interactive activity **to evaluate** which businesses add most value from alternatives. 2 - Take three products. Break the products down into their component parts – what raw materials were used and what other costs would have been incurred. Why are consumers prepared to pay the price for the product? What are the main ways the business adds value? 1	1 Student Book, Introduction to Small Business – Chapter 5 2 Active Teach

| 6 | **Topic 1.1 Spotting a business opportunity**

The options available in starting up a business. | To recognise that there are different options available in starting up a business.

To understand the main principles of a franchise.

To be able to state at least two advantages and two disadvantages of a franchise.

To recognise the importance of location in setting up a business. | - Case study on franchising to **calculate** the costs, **examine** the factors affecting the choice of franchise and **evaluate** which franchise a business should chose from two alternatives. 1

- Research existing franchsises to **compare** their advantages and disadvantages for the franchisee and franchisor. 1

- **Discuss** the Toni7Guy franchise from video material. 2

- Interactive activity to **understand** the potential advantages and disadvantages of franchising. 2

- **Examine** the factors affecting a franchisee, such as Rosemary Conley or Dominos Pizza. 4/7

- **Examine** the factors affecting choice of a franchise from a variety of articles relating to starting up in business via a franchise. 5/6/8 | 1 Student Book, Introduction to Small Business – Chapter 6

2 Active Teach

3 Business Active: Volume 1 Number 3. January 2006. Is franchising a good idea? pp14 – 16.

4 Business case studies – Case Study 10 – Rosemary Conley.

5 Bitesize Revision: Different types of business

6 eBus: Jan 2007 – Franchising.

7 Business Active: Volume 2 Number 1. September 2006: 'Delivering Pizza'

8 Startups – Start a Franchise: http://www.startups.co.uk/6678842909145602420/start-a-franchise.html |

7/8	**Topic 1.2 Showing enterprise** What is enterprise?	To be able to state at least 4 features of being enterprising. To understand the difference between a good and a service. To understand how mindmaps can be used by entrepreneurs to spot opportunities.	- Case studies on horse stables, a machine repair business and gift wrapping services to **understand** the skills required by entrepreneurs and **evaluate** to what extent entrepreneurs will be successful. 1 - Interactive activities to **analyse** the factors that make successful entrepreneurs, whether products are goods or services and the features of mindmaps. 2 - A series of activities involving starting a business. For example, make a list of the reasons why you think that a person might want to start up their own business. Put the reasons in an order of **priority** - the most important reason first down to the least important reason. Also, **design** a poster advertising the benefits of starting up a new business. Take into account that it needs to attract attention and include information that might be needed by those who might be thinking of starting up their own business. 3 - An enterprise task, based on a scenario where students are stranded on a desert island with few resources to **encourage thinking and creativity**. 5 - **Understand** the factors affecting business start-ups from articles. 4/7 - **Young enterprise programme** for students. 6	1 Student Book - Introduction to Small Business – Chapters 7, 12 and 14 2 Active Teach 3 What is Enterprise? Biz/ed: http://www.bized.co.uk/educators/level2/busactivity/lesson/enterprise1.htm 4 Business Active: Volume 1 Number 1. September 2005. Innovation and Enterprise, pp14 – 16. 5 eBus: October 2006 - Thinking 6 'Entrepreneurship Masterclass' run by Young Enterprise. See: www.young-enterprise.org.uk. 7 Startups – Entrepreneur Skills: http://www.startups.co.uk/6678842907515998169/entrepreneur-skills.html
9	**Topic 1.2 Showing enterprise** Being creative and enterprising.	To understand the role of creative thinking in business enterprise. To be able to identify key questions that entrepreneurs ask.	- Case studies on businesses making greeting cards and wedding albums **identifying** lateral and blue skies thinking and questions that entrepreneurs might ask and **evaluating** their importance. 1 - Interactive activities on thinking hats and questions that entrepreneurs ask. 2 - Thinking hats activity based on a circus that has to think creatively to solve a problem when a storm wrecks the circus tent. 3 - A useful activity to help students think creatively based on a business problem. 4 - Short exercises based on different problems/scenarios designed to encourage creative thinking. 5	1 Student Book - Introduction to Small Business – Chapters 8 and 9 2 Active Teach 3 eBus: Sept 2006. Deliberate Creativity. 4 eBus: September 2006. Penbrella – a business problem. 5 eBuss: November 2006. Unlock your creativity.

10	**Topic 1.2 Showing enterprise** Invention and Innovation	To be able to state clearly the difference between the two terms. To understand the steps that an entrepreneur can take to protect their ideas and products.	- Case study **identifying** innovation an invention, **examining** the benefits of patents and **evaluating** continued innovation. 1 - Interactive activity **explaining** the difference between invention and innovation. 2 - **Examine** how to protect inventions. 3 - A summary of a copyright dispute between Mattell and the makers of Bratz dolls over who owns the copyright for the design of the Bratz doll. 4 - **Debate** a variety of issues from articles, including some useful ones on copyright, patents and trademarks. 5	1 Student Book - Introduction to Small Business – Chapter 10 2 Active Teach 3 BBC: "Protecting your invention" http://news.bbc.co.uk/1/hi/business 4 Biz/ed In the News – Bratz dolls and copyright: http://www.bized.co.uk/cgi-bin/chron.pl?id=3245 5 Startups: Legal Issues: http://www.startups.co.uk/6678842910853900731/legal-issues.html
11	**Topic 1.2 Showing enterprise** Calculated risk	To recognise that business involves degrees of risk To appreciate that business can also bring rewards. To understand how to balance out the risk-reward ratio.	- Case study involving an engineering business, **identifying** upsides and downsides and **evaluating** success using calculated risk. 1 - Interactive activity **identifying** upsides and downsides of a decision. 2 - A series of resources looking at how businesses can measure success. 3 - A series of resources looking at what business failure means and the causes of business failure. 4 - A short case study on a business start-up and some of the issues that need to be considered. 5	1 Student Book - Introduction to Small Business – Chapter 11 2 Active Teach. 3 Biz/ed: Business Success and Failure 1: http://www.bized.co.uk/educators/level2/busactivity/lesson/success1.htm 4 Biz/ed: Business SJccess and Failure 2: http://www.bized.co.uk/educators/level2/busactivity/lesson/success2.htm 5 eBus: May 2007. Bernie's start-up.

12	**Topic 1.3 Putting a business idea into practice** Business objectives	To be able to state at least 3 financial and 3 non-financial objectives for starting up a business.	- Case study involving two chemists, **identifying** financial and non-financial objectives and **comparing** the objectives of the two businesses. 1 - Interactive activity **classifying** types of objectives. 2 - A mind map showing the overall issues relating to business objectives. 3 - Examining business objectives using case studies such as Fitness Friends. 4/5	1 Student book - Introduction to Small Business – Chapter 13 2 Active Teach. 3 Biz/ed – Business Objectives Mind map: http://www.bized.co.uk/educators/16-19/business/strategy/presentation/busobjectives2map.htm 4 Bitesize Revision: Business objectives – pp20 – 21. 5 Business case studies – Case Study 8 – Fitness Friends.
13/14	**Topic 1.3 Putting a business idea into practice** Costs and revenues	To state a definition of revenue, fixed costs, variable cost, price, total cost and profit. To state two ways in which a new business might forecast sales.	- Case study of a pet cleaning service involving the **calculation** of costs, revenues and profit. 1 - Spreadsheets **calculating** of revenue and costs. 2 - Interactive activity **calculating** costs and revenues. 2 - **Discuss** how fixed and variable costs change using graphs and an animation. 2 - A short case study on costs and revenues relating to a Chinese takeaway business. 3 - **Discuss** setting turnover targets. 4 - Case study **analysing** improving revenue and profit and profit of Sainsbury's. 5 Note – break-even is not on this part of the specification, but this resource can be useful in introducing students to cost, revenue and profit concepts.	1 Student book - Introduction to Small Business – Chapter 15 2 Active Teach. 3 eBus: 2005. The Ho-li takeaway. 4 BBC: 'How to set a turnover target': http://news.bbc.co.uk/1/hi/business 5 Biz/ed: Break –even. http://www.bized.co.uk/educators/level2/finance/activity/breakeven21.htm

15/16	Topic 1.3 Putting a business idea into practice			
	Cash flow	To understand the difference between cash flow and profit.	- Case study of a t-shirt maker **calculating** cash flow. 1	1 Student book - Introduction to Small Business – Chapters 16 and 17.
		To understand the difference between a cash flow forecast and a cash flow statement.	- Case study involving a travel agency, **explaining** the uses of a business plan. 1 - Spreadsheets **calculating** of cash flow. 2	2 Active Teach. 3 GCSE Business Studies Bitesize Revision: Cash flow – pp 39 – 41.
		To be able to complete a cash flow forecast table.	- A series of resources that include practical activities based around **cash flow forecasting** using a small business selling fruit as a context. - **Cash flow forecasting** exercises. 4	4 Biz/ed: Cash flow. http://www.bized.co.uk/educators/level2/finance/lesson/cashflow1.htm
		To identify at least four factors that affect cash flow.	- A large scale **simulation** that enables students to input details into a cash flow forecast and 'run' a business for a year responding to possible changes in circumstances which affect cash flow. 5	5 Biz/ed Cash flow simulation: http://www.bized.co.uk/learn/business/accounting/cashflow/simulation/index.htm
		To understand how poor cash flow can lead to business failure.	- **Estimating** and **evaluating** cash flow using a case study. 6	6 Business case studies – Case Study 26 – Peterborough United FC.
		To understand the use of the business plan in planning cash flow.	- **Analysing** the features of a good business plan. 7	7 BBC news http://news.bbc.co.uk/1/hi/business/2943252.stm

			Resources
17	**Topic 1.3 Putting a business idea into practice** Obtaining finance	To be able to state at least three different sources of finance for a new business. To recognise the difference between short-term finance and long-term finance.	- Case study of a manufacturer of drilling equipment **examining** reasons for obtaining finance and **evaluating** appropriate sources. 1 - Interactive activity **examining the most appropriate** sources of finance for a business. 2 - A series of tasks and activities looking at different ways in which businesses can raise finance both for start-ups and for running the business. For example, consider how **changes in interest rates** affect repayments and **assess** the suitability of different types of short and long term finance 3 - Examine **specific advice** from Business Link on how to raise finance. 4 - Links to a variety of articles relating to ways of obtaining business finance. 5 - Case study **examining** the type of finance raised by Tumble Tots. 6 - **Discuss** how finance can be raised in different ways from articles. 7	1 Student book - Introduction to Small Business – Chapter 18 2 Active Teach. 3 Biz/ed: Sources of finance for business: http://www.bized.co.uk/educators/level2/finance/lesson/sources1.htm 4 Business Link: Finance and Grants: http://www.businesslink.gov.uk/bdotg/action/layer?topicId=1073858790&r.lc=en&r.s=m 5 Startups – Business Financing. http://www.startups.co.uk/6678842909123868795/business-financing.html 6 Business case studies – Case Study 30 – Tumble Tots. 7 BBC: Raising Finance: http://news.bbc.co.uk/1/hi/business
18	**Topic 1.4 Making the start-up effective** Customer focus and marketing mix	Understand that a focus on the needs of the customer are essential to business success. To recognise the main elements of the marketing mix. To be able to identify key elements of the marketing mix in different contexts.	- Case study of a clothing designer **examining** the factors that may affect its marketing mix and **evaluating** if the mix would change if the business was different. 1 - Interactive activity **placing elements of the market mix** into a mindmap. 2 - **Presentation** that can be edited – covers the 7Ps. 3 - Activity considering how elements of the marketing mix are **stressed** by different companies – based on larger companies but can be adapted to suit small businesses. 4	1 Student book - Introduction to Small Business – Chapter 19 2 Active Teach. 3 Biz/ed Presentation: The Marketing Mix http://www.bized.co.uk/educators/16-19/business/marketing/presentation/mix.ppt 4 Biz/ed: Marketing Mix Activity: http://www.bized.co.uk/educators/16-19/business/marketing/activity/mix.htm

19	**Topic 1.4 Making the start-up effective**	To understand the principle of liability.	- Case study **examining** the advantages or not of limited liability for a scaffold service. 1	1 Student book - Introduction to Small Business – Chapter 20
	Limited liability	To be able to state the difference between limited and unlimited liability.	- Interactive activity **comparing** the benefits of limited and unlimited liability. 2	2 Active Teach.
			- **Discussion** of the effects of a limited liability of a sole trader and a limited company using video material. 2	3 Biz/ed: Notes on Limited Liability: http://www.bized.co.uk/learn/economics/notes/liability.htm
		To appreciate how the extent of liability can influence decision-making on the type of business organisation chosen by an entrepreneur.	- Set of **notes** and accompanying **mindmap** on the principle of limited liability. 3	4 Startups – Setting up a company: http://www.startups.co.uk/6678842911461046207/setting-up-a-company.html
			- **Guidelines** on setting up as different types of business organisation. 4	

| 20 | **Topic 1.4 Making the start-up effective**

Start up legal and tax issues | To recognise the importance of an appropriate trading name for a business.

To appreciate why accurate record keeping is important to a business.

To understand the main taxes a small business will have to pay – VAT, corporation tax, income tax and National Insurance contributions. | - Case study of a computer repair service **explaining** why business must keep records and **evaluating** the suitability of the choice of business name. 1

- Interactive activity **considering** taxes paid by businesses. 2

- One of a series of business profiles **examining** a variety of aspects of running a business. This looks at a small hairdressing business in the South West of England. 3

- A case study **examining** a small business selling spectacles. 4

- A case study with accompanying **worksheet and interactive quiz.** 5

- Official **guidelines** on the taxes that businesses have to pay. 6

- Series of **links** offering advice to small businesses. Specific advice from Business Link on taxes, returns and payroll. 7

- **Scenario** based around a business person who has not paid their taxes. 8 | 1 Student book - Introduction to Small Business – Chapter 21

2 Active Teach.

3 Biz/ed Business Profiles: No 31 Hair and Beauty. http://www.bized.co.uk/compfact/no31/no31index.htm

4 Biz/ed: Sepextacular http://www.bized.co.uk/compfact/spex/spexindex.htm

5 Biz/ed: Business Planning Case Study: http://www.bized.co.uk/virtual/bank/business/planning/case study.htm

6 Her Majesty's Revenue & Customs (HMR&C) – information for businesses on tax issues: http://www.hmrc.gov.uk/businesses/index.shtml

7 Business Link – Small Business advice: http://www.businesslink.gov.uk/bdotg/action/layer?r.ll=1073858781&topicId=1073858805&r.lc=en&r.s=m

http://www.businesslink.gov.uk/bdotg/action/layer?r.ll=1073858805&topicId=1073858808&r.lc=en&r.s=m

8 eBus: December 2006. A mess: 5 days to pay. |

21	**Topic 1.4 Making the start-up effective** Customer satisfaction	To give a definition of customer satisfaction and customer service. To be able to state at least three benefits to a business of high levels of customer service. To be able to understand the importance of repeat business and how customer service and customer satisfaction play a role in securing repeat business.	- Case study of a plumber **explaining** the factors leading to customer satisfaction and **evaluating** customer service. 1 - Interactive activity **assessing** the features of good customer service. 2	1 Student book - Introduction to Small Business – Chapter 22 2 Active Teach.
22	**Topic 1.4 Making the start-up effective** Recruitment	To understand the key stages in recruiting employees to a business. To understand that both skills and attitude are important in the selection process. To appreciate that employing staff is governed by laws relating to race, sex, age and disability.	- Case study **considering** how legal factors affect recruitment in a car conversion business. 1 - Interactive activity **placing** the stages in the recruitment and selection process in order. - A resource taking students **step by step** through the recruitment process including a role play related to interviews and selection. 3 - **Specific advice** from Business Link on issues related to employing people. 4 - A **practical lesson** idea on the role of training in the workplace. 5 - **Consider** the recruitment process at the AA. The AA is a large organisation but this case study usefully highlights the role of apprenticeships in recruitment. 6	1 Student book - Introduction to Small Business – Chapter 23 2 Active Teach. 3 Biz/ed: Recruiting staff: http://www.bized.co.uk/educators/16-19/business/hrm/lesson/recruit1.htm 4 Business Link: Employing people: http://www.businesslink.gov.uk/bdotg/action/layer?r.l1=1073858808&topicId=1073858787&r.lc=en&r.s=m 5 Teaching Business and Economics – the EBEA Journal. Spring 2007. Training – illustrating the benefits. Pp18 – 19. 6 Business case studies – Case Study 36 – The AA.

23	Topic 1.5 Understanding the economic context	To understand that a market is made up of buyers and sellers.	- Case study **examining** how changes in price affect demand for and supply of steel parts. 1	1 Student book - Introduction to Small Business – Chapter 24
	Demand and supply	To understand that the price of a good is determined by the interaction of demand and supply.	- Interactive activity **classifying** types of goods.	2 Active Teach.
		To recognise that a shortage will lead to a rise in price and a surplus to a fall in price.	- A number of different types of activity covering the nature and functioning of markets including **interactive tasks, animations,** a **word search** and a **drag and drop** activity. 3	3 Biz/ed: The nature of markets: http://www.bized.co.uk/educators/level2/markets/lesson/markets1.htm
		To be able to recognise the difference between a goods market and a commodity market.		
		To appreciate that changes in commodity prices can affect small businesses.		

	Topic	Objectives	Activities	Resources
24/25/26	**Topic 1.5 Understanding the economic context**			
	Interest rates	To understand that interest is the payment made for a loan/received for savings.	- Case study of an electrical retailer **explaining** the effect of changes in interest rates on the business and **evaluating** how it might react. 1 - Interactive activity **examining the effect of changes** in interest rates. 2	1 Student book - Introduction to Small Business – Chapter 25 2 Active Teach. 3 Biz/ed: The economic context of business: http://www.bized.co.uk/educators/level2/external/lesson/context1.htm Biz/ed: External influences – interest rates. http://www.bized.co.uk/educators/level2/external/activity/influence11.htm
		To understand how changes in interest rates can affect small businesses.	- A series of resources **examining** the main factors that affect a business including economic growth, the business cycle, employment and unemployment and inflation. 3	
	Exchange rates	To understand that the exchange rate is the price of acquiring a foreign currency.	- Case study of a frozen food manufacturer **examining** how changes in the value of the pound can affect the business and **evaluating** the extent of this effect. 1	1 Student book - Introduction to Small Business – Chapter 26 2 Active Teach. 3 Biz/ed: International Business – business and exchange rates: http://www.bized.co.uk/educators/level2/international/lesson/business2.htm Biz/ed: External influences – exchange rates. http://www.bized.co.uk/educators/level2/external/activity/influence14.htm
		To be able to calculate simple exchange rate conversions using dollars, pounds and euro.	- Interactive activity **examining the effect of changes** in exchange rates on imports and exports. 2 - A resource in four sections which **examines** the role of exchange rates in business. 3	4 eBus: March 2007. Going straight.
		To understand that changes in exchange rates affect buyers from abroad and sellers to foreign countries differently.	- Case study of a company called Beautiful Vending Ltd covering issues such as cash flow and exchange rates. 4	

BUSINESS

	Topic	Learning objectives	Activities	Resources
27	**Topic 1.5 Understanding the economic context** Business cycle	To provide a definition of 'economic activity'. To be able to recognise that the level of economic activity changes over time. To be able to state how different stages in the business cycle might affect different small businesses.	- Case study **examining** how change sin economic activity affect a supplier of parts for mechanical diggers. 1 - Interactive activity **considering how business activity in the UK** has changed in recent years. 2 - A series of resources **examining** the main factors that affect a business including economic growth, the business cycle, employment and unemployment and inflation. 3	1 Student book - Introduction to Small Business – Chapter 27 2 Active Teach. 3 Biz/ed: The economic context of business: http://www.bized.co.uk/educators/level2/external/lesson/context1.htm
28	**Topic 1.5 Understanding the economic context** Stakeholders	To provide a definition of the term 'stakeholder'. To be able to recognise the key stakeholders in a number of small business contexts. To be able to state the basic rights and responsibilities of different stakeholders. To understand and identify at least five possible areas of conflict between stakeholders in a business.	- Case study **explaining** the stakeholders of a house maintenance service. 1 - Interactive activity **examining** how a stakeholders of a recycling service are **affected** by the business. 2 - A resource looking at the rights and responsibilities of stakeholders and how conflicts can arise as a result of business decisions and the way that these can be resolved. 3 - Lesson ideas to develop a practical understanding of the interests of different stakeholder groups. 4 - Stakeholders at BSkyB. The focus here is on a large business but the context might be useful to help students to **understand** the main groups of stakeholders. 5	1 Student book - Introduction to Small Business – Chapter 28 2 Active Teach. 3 Biz/ed: Knowing your Stakeholders. http://www.bized.co.uk/educators/level2/busactivity/lesson/knowing1.htm 4 Teaching Business and Economics – the EBEA Journal. Summer 2007. Stakeholders – do you have a voice? Pp14 – 17. 5 Business case studies – Case Study 7 – BSkyB.

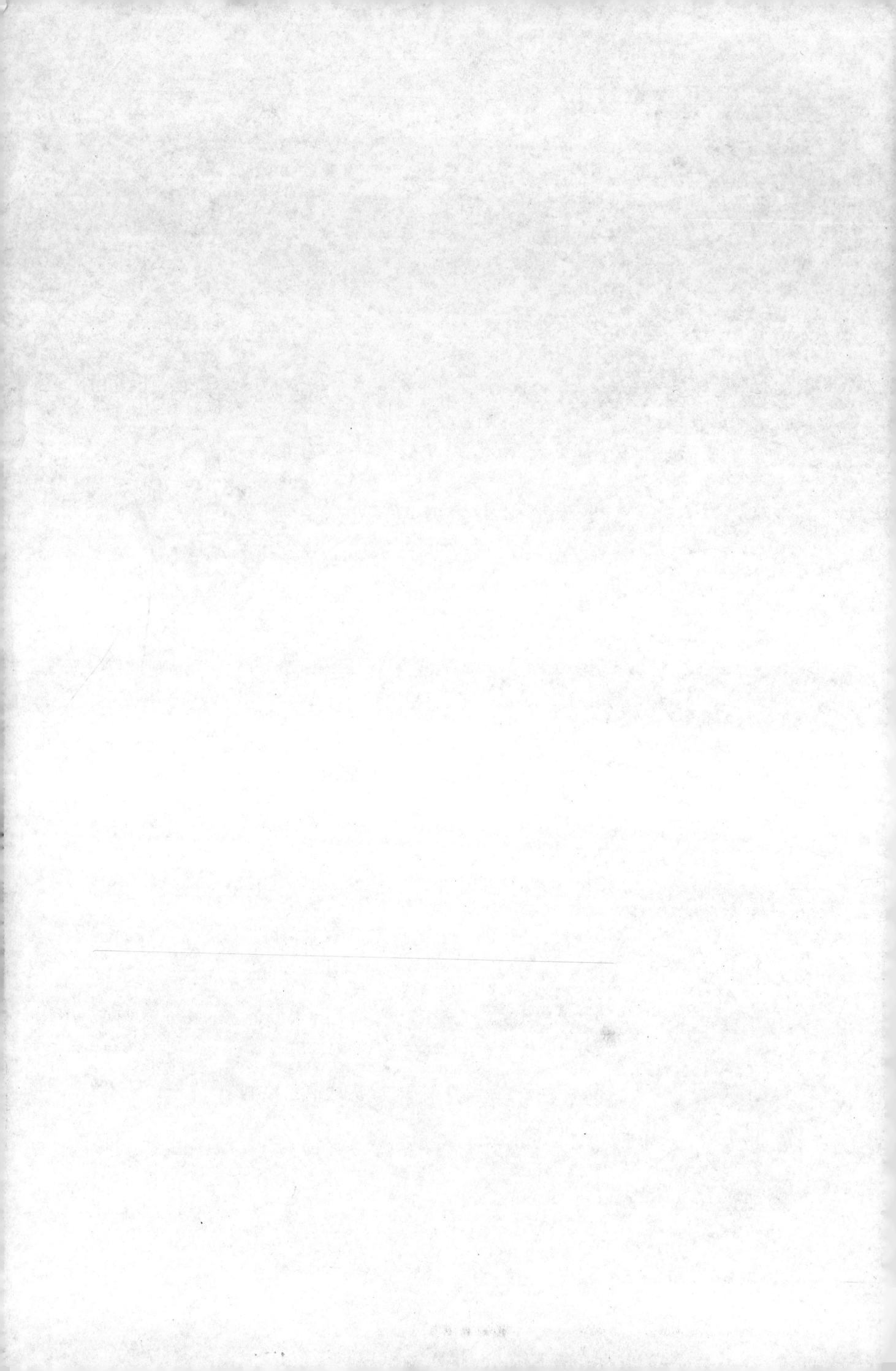